SpringerBriefs in Business

T0215155

More information about this series at http://www.springer.com/series/8860

Vissanu Zumitzavan · Jonathan Michie

Personal Knowledge Management, Leadership Styles, and Organisational Performance

A Case Study of the Healthcare Industry in Thailand

 Springer

Vissanu Zumitzavan
The College of Local Administration,
   Khon Kaen University
Khon Kaen
Thailand

Jonathan Michie
University of Oxford
Oxford
UK

ISSN 2191-5482   ISSN 2191-5490   (electronic)
SpringerBriefs in Business
ISBN 978-981-287-437-5   ISBN 978-981-287-438-2   (eBook)
DOI 10.1007/978-981-287-438-2

Library of Congress Control Number: 2015932625

Springer Singapore Heidelberg New York Dordrecht London

Printed on acid-free paper

Springer Science+Business Media Singapore Pte Ltd. is part of Springer Science+Business Media (www.springer.com)

Acknowledgments

The accomplishment of this research was made possible through the support of several individuals and groups. First, Vissanu would like to show his indebtedness to Prof. Jonathan Michie, and Associate Professor Titinun Aumnuay, for their prosperity of ideas and guidances in inspiring to acquire an insightful notion to develop this book. In addition, great thankfulness is owed to Vissanu's parents, Mr. Sompoch Zumitzavan and Mrs. Daungyiva Zumitzavan, for their unending support throughout every stage of life.

Finally, we would like to say thanks to the respondents of this research, the top management of the healthcare industry in Thailand for their participations in providing invaluable data and to Khon Kaen University, Khon Kaen, Thailand, for the scholarship to conduct this research.

Vissanu Zumitzavan
Jonathan Michie

Contents

Abstract

This research scrutinises the connection between the demographics of respondents, their personal knowledge management (PKM) skills, their leadership styles and the performance and size of their organisations; it investigates to what degree the PKM and leadership styles of top management are advantageous to the healthcare industry. Survey questionnaires were distributed to 1,000 top managers of hospitals in Thailand, and responses were received from 539. Various statistical techniques were applied to test our hypotheses, including descriptive statistics, correlations and multiple regression analysis. Results indicate that PKM and leadership styles are statistically associated with positive organisational performance. The findings also show that the relationship between PKM and organisational performance is mediated by the leadership styles.

Chapter 1
Introduction

1.1 Introduction

Organisations or companies are currently encountering a variety of business challenges. Globalisation has generated both new opportunities and difficulties (Michie 2011). Large organisations with a vigorous history can no longer compete unless they keep changing themselves to suit different trends (Marcel and Rajiv 2012).

Competition in the global market is complex, and top management capable of competing successfully in this context are indispensable to their businesses (Hagen and Lodha 2004). Specific sectors have individual problems; for example, in the healthcare industry, Eiff (2012) proposed that the spread of chronic diseases and severe illnesses are causing an increasing demand for medical services. This is especially true in developing countries, where patients are becoming more demanding (Kanji and Moura e Sá 2003). They expect not only reliable medicine, but also a remarkable healing environment (Chen et al. 2011; Yun 2013). By observing organisational performance in the light of competitive advantage, any organisation can adapt itself to the changing business environment with even limited resources if they are valuable, rare, inimitable and non-substitutable (Barney 2001). Such organisations could be considered as gaining a competitive advantage. Although not all organisations in the healthcare industry are capable of satisfying all customers' needs or improving organisational performance, those capable of achieving greater levels of competitive advantage can achieve different levels of organisational performance (Reeleder et al. 2006).

Wright (2007) argues that organisational performance is increasingly being determined by the contributions of knowledge workers. These knowledge workers are people with a high level of expertise, education and experience, whose primary

© The Author(s) 2015
V. Zumitzavan and J. Michie, *Personal Knowledge Management, Leadership Styles, and Organisational Performance*, SpringerBriefs in Business, DOI 10.1007/978-981-287-438-2_1

role involves the creation, distribution or application of knowledge. Academic scholars have proposed that the concept of organisational learning has positive impacts on enhancing organisational performance (Neuendorf 2002; Szarka et al. 2004), in which the top management encourages a learning environment within their organisations; knowledge needs to be shared at every level of the organisation (Sosik et al. 2011).

In this knowledge era, various types of organisations are struggling to manage the collective correlation between PKM and organisational knowledge management. If an individual becomes productive through PKM, the organisation may benefit (Semertzaki 2011). The concept of Knowledge Management (KM) has been widely known for decades, and PKM is considered to be an offshoot. However, Pauleen (2009), Tsui (2002) and Zhang (2009) suggest that PKM is still under-explored. Cheong and Tsui (2011) concluded that search counts reported at September 2009 revealed that PKM was interchangeable with Knowledge Management. Although KM is concerned with transferring knowledge at different stages and tends to be of most use to the organisation, PKM continues to play a vital role in encouraging learning within the organisation.

More importantly, scholars have emphasised that PKM, leadership styles and performance are crucial and interrelated variables contributing to organisational performance, and thus there is a critical need to examine these relationships (Hadikin and O'Driscoll 2000; Plsek and Wilson 2001; Tepper 2000; Harris et al. 2007). As such, PKM can be recognised as a classification of knowledge management elaborated within different management boundaries through carrying out day-to-day responsibilities, and also influencing leadership styles to ensure the greatest impact on improving organisational performance. Thus, appropriate PKM may involve the factors for creating and encouraging leadership styles, which in turn could improve organisational performance overall.

The aim of this research is to investigate which types of PKM and leadership styles are supportive to the organisation. The healthcare industry in Thailand was taken as the unit of analysis, building on our previous study of leadership styles and organisational outcomes for the motor-tyre industry in Thailand (Michie and Zumitzavan 2012). Like other ASEAN countries, Thailand is facing challenges which have been acknowledged ever since the ASEAN summit of 2003, with the establishment of the ASEAN Economic Community (AEC) in 2015 to encourage the free association of commodities, services, investments and capital (Hew and Soesastro 2003). Nearly all member countries are preparing to be equipped to acquire the most advantages out of the AEC. In addition, various industries are shaping their strategies to deal with imminent expansion. Thailand's healthcare industry is the focus of this research since its development will affect various aspects of national competitiveness. According to data from Thailand's Ministry of

Public Health (MOPH), in 2006 there were 997 state owned hospitals in the country, composed of 25 general hospitals, 70 provincial and district hospitals, 727 community hospitals, 58 hospitals under different departments of MOPH and 117 hospitals outside MOPH. An additional 471 private hospitals are listed by the Association of Thai Private Hospitals. Thus, the population of our research interest is 1,468 hospitals throughout Thailand. One of the most commonly used formulas for determining sample size is by Krejcie and Morgan (1970). Their table shows that for a population size of 1,500, a sample size of no less than 306 is recommended (see Table A-22 in Appendices). In this research the sample is 539, a satisfactory level according to Krejcie and Morgan's formula.

1.2 Research Objectives

This study aimed to investigate and clarify the extent to which PKM is encouraged in the organisation and to determine the supportive leadership styles of healthcare's top management. Hence, there are three objectives:

1. To investigate the relationship between PKM, leadership styles and organisational performance.
2. To ascertain whether there is a mediation effect between PKM, leadership and organisational performance.
3. To provide recommendations on how to improve organisational performance through effective PKM and leadership styles.

1.3 Scope of the Research

This research is determined to scrutinise the influence of PKM and different styles of leadership of top management on organisational performance in the healthcare industry in the Thai context. The mediation effects were also tested to understand the extent to which the relationship between independent and dependent variables may be mediated when the independent variables are the demographics of respondents and their PKM and leadership styles, and the dependent variable is organisational performance.

For this research, healthcare organisations were selected as samples and data collected from the directors or top managements by survey questionnaires. Descriptive statistics, correlations and hierarchical multiple regression analysis were applied to test hypotheses (Fig. 1.1).

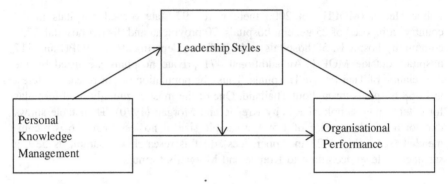

Fig. 1.1 Conceptual framework

1.4 Organisation of the Research

This research comprises five chapters. This chapter presents the justification for and an overview of the research. Related literature is reviewed in Chap. 2. The research methodology is explained in Chap. 3 with a discussion of the approaches applied to analyse the data. Chapter 4 shows the results of the quantitative data analysis, and Chap. 5 discusses the findings, considers the implications and makes recommendations. Chapter 6 concludes findings of research overall.

1.5 Conclusion

This chapter presented the rationale for the research, and described the motivation for selecting the healthcare industry in Thailand for the empirical investigation; the research questions and objectives were defined. The methodology of the research was explained concisely to elucidate the approaches to analysing the data. Finally, the structure of this research was highlighted, to guide the readers through the processes and findings of the research.

The literature of PKM, leadership styles and organisational performance is reviewed in the following chapter.

Chapter 2
Literature Review and Conceptual Framework

2.1 Introduction

This chapter presents the key literature relevant to the concept of PKM, leadership styles and organisational performance and discusses the connections and variations highlighted by existing researchers and their empirical findings to emphasise the concepts explored in this research.

2.1.1 Personal Knowledge Management

Different cultures produce different learning environments from different levels of individual and organisational learning, and researchers have indicated that Asian, American and other Western top management have created various levels of learning in their organisations, resulting in different levels of organisational performance (Hofstede 1998; Waldman et al. 2006). Hence, to understand the various ways in which top management manage and transfer knowledge within their organisation, it is necessary to explore how individuals encourage their organisational members to participate in the organisation (Avery et al. 2001; McVanel-Viney 2008). Knowledge management typically emphasises organisational knowledge (Pauleen 2009).

Several researchers on KM have studied the organisational level (Pauleen 2009; Tsui 2002; Zhang et al. 2002). Thus, in recognising the management disciplines from individual to organisational learning there remains room to investigate (Wilson et al. 2008; Semertzaki 2011). Over recent decades there has been little research in this field, although several scholars have attempted to define PKM, including Frand and Hixon (1999), Avery et al. (2001), Higgison (2004), Jefferson (2006), Volkel and Abecker (2008), Martin (2008) and Jarche (2010). Frand and Hixon (1999) said that PKM is a structure premeditated for individual purposes, a conceptual framework to

© The Author(s) 2015
V. Zumitzavan and J. Michie, *Personal Knowledge Management, Leadership Styles, and Organisational Performance*, SpringerBriefs in Business,
DOI 10.1007/978-981-287-438-2_2

organise and incorporate data that individuals feel is essential so that it becomes part of their personal knowledge base. It provides a strategy for transforming what may be unsystematic pieces of information into particular groupings which can be analytically applied and extend personal knowledge; this is particularly true in the healthcare industry (Dunne and Kelliher 2013).

Avery et al. (2001) and Wiggins (2013) proposed different views and suggested that PKM could be a form of individually developed self-awareness of their limits and capabilities, i.e. what individuals know and what individuals could perform. This personal self-awareness is an understanding of how much individuals know, and how to access the things individuals distinguish. From the vast amount of data available and the various means for acquiring new data, each individual maps out his or her own areas of expertise and own methods for specific learning.

Higgison (2004) considered PKM as 'a concept of facilitating personal knowledge and data so that it is manageable, meaningful and valuable to the individuals; maintaining networks, interactions and communities; making individuals' day-to-day responsibilities simpler and more gratifying, and exploiting personal capital'.

Jefferson (2006) stressed that 'PKM is focused on a bottom-up method, with an individual perspective to KM'. The aim is to make it possible for individuals to select what information to possess, how to organise it and who to exchange it with. Individuals are supposed to be able to manage their own information for full use in a meaningful and available form when needed. PKM enables organisational members to arrange both soft and hard contents in such a way as to enable them to make sense of the accumulation they are continually seeking for. However, Volkel and Abecker (2008) pointed out that PKM 'denote[s] the process of the individuals to manage knowledge' and 'it deals with embodied and encoded knowledge i.e. mostly with personal, self-authored artefacts'.

Martin (2008) describes it thus: 'PKM is knowledge individuals contain and how individuals can manage it, mobilise it and apply it to accomplish individuals' goals, and how individuals can continue to practise knowledge'. Jarche (2010) suggests that 'PKM is an individual, disciplined practise by which one makes sense of data, reflection and awareness. In the past this may include keeping journals, writing letters, or involving in conversation. These are still effective, but with digital media individuals may be able to add contexts by classifying, noting or even revising it. Individual may also store digital media for easy retrieval'.

Drucker (1998) argued that knowledge workers have positive effects on economic growth. This involves individual decision-making and actions (Ramírez and Nembhard 2004). As suggested by Pauleen (2009), PKM is a process of self-development; the individual is crucial in encouraging a learning environment, supported by organisational learning and knowledge management. Nonaka (1991) proposed that new knowledge generally arises from individuals. Thus, organisations contribute by promoting, developing, valuing and managing its employees as individuals (Swan et al. 1999).

Ahmed et al. (2002) argue that PKM comprises individuals linking and distributing their experience, skills, intuitions, ideas, judgments, contexts, motivations and interpretations. Efimova (2004) defined PKM as 'an approach that complements organisational knowledge management by concentrating on approaches to sustain productivity of an individual knowledge organisational member'. It is also considered a tool furnishing knowledge workers with mandatory skills to manage their individual knowledge. Pauleen (2009) also recommended that in the world of the knowledge-driven society, it has widely become indispensable for individuals to maintain, develop and contribute their skills to prepare themselves for any possibility of competitive advantage in the market.

Finally, the PKM skill model of Avery et al. (2001) identified seven information skills: (1) retrieving, (2) evaluating, (3) organising, (4) collaborating, (5) analysing, (6) presenting and (7) securing, as follows:

2.1.2 Retrieving Information

This involves collecting data not just from print and electronic sources, but through experimentation and oral enquiry, as well as a wide range of more discipline-specific practices. Low-tech skills such as raising questions, taking notes, using search tools and reading are required. Also, as the literature on information literacy emphasises, considerable effort should be put into framing the enquiry even before information retrieval commences. The practical use of Internet search engines and electronic databases in the enquiry process requires technology skills. It is challenging to clarify the required information influencing new knowledge establishment and it is necessary to be familiar with keyword and subject searching to widen and narrow the scope of the search (Alexopoulos and Buckley 2013).

2.1.3 Evaluating Information

This is closely related to the skills of retrieving information. Strategies for information retrieval are based on selecting and evaluating data. However, evaluation also takes place after retrieval, as the quality and relevance of various portions of information relate to the problem at hand (Pauleen 2009). It is noted that different areas of study are likely to place emphasis on different criteria. The greater availability of information in the current information-rich environment imposes on these skills far greater importance in the technological era (Porter 1997). The intelligent use of some crude electronic tools, such as 'relevance indicator', can be relevant to the effective evaluation of information, requiring the effective evaluation of the quality and the relevance of information gathered (Dorsey 2001).

2.1.4 Organising Information

Frand and Hixon (1999) agreed that the skill of organising information is a core section of the enquiry practice, concentrating on constructing the links necessary to connect pieces of information to give them meaning. Techniques for organising information help the enquirer to overcome some of the limitations of the human information processing system. In some ways, the key challenge in organising information is for the enquirer to use connecting principles linking new information with old information (Evans and Qureshi 2013). Familiarity with technological skills is crucial in the application of electronic tools including directories and folders, databases, web pages and web portals to make connections (Avery et al. 2001).

This organising skill is to improve practices enabling individual knowledge workers to develop strategies consistent with the nature of their duties, with their learning capabilities and with relationships they may have (Dorsey 2001). Skills are also required to apply technologies such as databases, websites and applications to store the information in the system (Porter 1997).

2.1.5 Collaborating Information

Practical collaborative work includes the underlying principles of listening, showing respect for the understanding of others' ideas, developing and following through on shared practices, building win/win relationships and resolving conflicts. With collaborative enquiry, partners need to learn to share ideas (Ghaznavi et al. 2011). The availability of new electronic tools for collaboration to support both synchronous and asynchronous communication requires an entire new collection of practices for efficient information exchange. This skill influences the utilising of information in linking others with respective and shared practices. It requires the understanding of communication among organisational members (Herghiligiu et al. 2013).

2.1.6 Analysing Information

This is essential to the process of transforming information into knowledge. At the same time, it is the most discipline-specific information skill, since the models, theories and frameworks central to analysis are frequently involved in academic disciplines (Kelly 2006). Analysis involves organisation of information, but goes further in its emphasis on the importance of respect for standards in public communities. These skills address the challenges of extracting meaning out of data. In some disciplines, electronic tools such as spreadsheets and statistical software provide the means to analyse information, but the human element is central in enclosing the model embodied in that software. The challenge is to distinguish meaningful information from data (Suresh 2014). These skills require the ability to convert knowledge into various usable forms.

2.1.7 Presenting Information

The key to the presentation of information is the audience; this means, as in the case of analysing information, that understanding disciplinary communities, their norms and standards is of core significance. An effective presentation takes into account not only an understanding of the listeners, but a rich consideration of the purposes of the presentation as it relates to them. The history and theory of rhetoric provides an abundant literature for supervision in the exercise of these skills. The emergence of new electronic tools and venues for presentations, through computer-based presentation tools and websites, makes attention to these information skills even more imperative (Świgoń 2013).

It is important to realise the purposes of the presentation as it directly affects the audience (Dorsey 2001). Beyond preparing professional-looking PowerPoint slides, the presenter needs to understand the behaviour and characteristics of audiences: Who they are, what information they require, from what perspective they interpret the information and how they make use of the information offered (Zhen et al. 2011).

2.1.8 Securing Information

Although this may sometimes be overlooked as an information skill (Dorsey 2001), Avery et al. (2001) endorsed it by affirming that it is strongly related to intellectual property issues and the multiplicity of security issues originating from the explosion of electronically networked environments. Securing information entails developing and implementing practices to ensure the confidentiality, integrity and actual existence of information, and it is crucial in answering a high level of intellectual property issues (Young 2012). The importance of keeping information secure is, indeed, built on the concept of intellectual property (Alexopoulos and Buckley 2013; Cheong and Tsui 2011; Ghaznavi et al. 2011; Kelly 2006).

PKM involves not only the contributions of individuals or organisational members but also relates to their knowledge, motivation and commitment (Dyer and Hatch 2006; Carrillo and Anumba 2002; Farrell 2006; Langhammer et al. 1993). Additionally, in the increasingly multicultural environment of organisations, top management may need to understand their own PKM in order to encourage individuals to participate in creating a learning environment and improve organisational performance (Clarke 2006; Dabbagh and Kitsantas 2012; Jung et al. 2007; Pirró et al. 2010; Wiggins 2013). Subsequently, it is clear that PKM is the process of how one perceives and transfers knowledge.

2.1.9 Leadership Styles

Scholars have proposed that a high-performance organisation requires first-class leadership; there is no simple solution and no rapid fix to compensate for poor leadership (Bell 2006; Künzle et al. 2010; Spinelli 2006). The concept of leadership has become increasingly familiar in discourses on management development over the last 20 years (Mumford and Gold 2004, p. 9). Bryman (1986) and Carter (2009) proposed that leadership has a variety of definitions, and there is no general agreement.

For instance, Stogdill (1948) claimed leadership describes the influence relationship that exists between top management and subordinates who intend real changes and outcomes which reflect their shared purpose. Rauch and Behling (1984) defined leadership as the process of influencing the activities of an organised group towards goal achievement. Similarly, Yukl (1989) proposed that leadership takes place among people; it involves the use of influence and is used to attain goals. Jaques and Clement (1991) suggested that leadership is the process through which an individual establishes the purpose or direction for individuals or a group of people, and encourages them to move along together with him or her and with each other in that direction, with competence and full commitment. Shackleton (1995, p. 2) explained leadership as the technique by which an individual influences organisational members towards the attainment of organisational goals.

Elaborating on the leadership role, Goleman (2000) proclaimed it may consist of generating outlines, establishing direction, aligning and motivating people as well as encouraging collaborative working, and producing positive and dramatic change. Thus, leadership may be defined as the progression by which a person acting as top management is accountable with distinctive responsibility for a wide range of tasks attained primarily through the exertions of other organisational members (Bowditch and Buono 2000). As such, Daft (2000) recommended that leadership involved an ability to encourage organisational members towards the attainment of goals (p. 502). Bedeian and Hunt (2006) recommended that leadership is a subset of management, and both are important to facilitate organisational performance. Nonetheless, Shriberg et al. (2005, p. 138) agreed that although leadership may be observed as part of the management pie, 'there is a good part of leadership that cannot be considered a subset of management'.

Generally, leadership could be defined as the capability of top management to encourage their members to generate exertion superior to their normal level of performance, which ultimately could contribute to improved organisational performance; in particular, several academic articles have acknowledged that leadership is expedient for effective development in the healthcare industry (Cooney et al. 2002; Butow et al. 2006; Hamlin 2005).

It could be argued that organisational learning is capable of continual regeneration as a result of the variety of knowledge, experience and skills of individuals within a culture where mutual questioning is encouraged and challenged around a shared purpose or vision (Johnson and Scholes 2002). Hence, to increase organisational performance, the organisation needs to explore new ways and instantaneously exploit what has been learned. In this respect, exploration is defined as variance-seeking and includes the constructs of creativity and innovation, whereas exploitation is reliability-seeking and includes the learning of standard routines, transfer of existing knowledge and incremental variation (Lewin et al. 1999; March 1991; Tushman et al. 2002).

The top management thus plays a key role in transferring knowledge and encouraging the learning environment in the organisation (Handy 1995). For this reason, the skills of an individual can encourage contributions from the collective responsibilities of organisational members who need to be well-developed and willing to practise the imperative skills being transferred (Carter 2009). The sorts of change needed in the creation of organisational learning are extremely challenging and need 'real leadership' (Senge 2010). Arguably, it appears that leadership plays an important role in shaping and maintaining organisational culture (Lok et al. 2005; Schein 1993).

Furthermore, the literature is undecided about how leadership is formed. There have been wide-ranging discussions on whether leadership is derived from 'nature' or 'nurture': Are individuals born as leaders, or trained in leadership (Shriberg and Shriberg 2011)? Grint (1991) suggested that leadership may refer to the ability and skills to intervene in new situations regardless of previous experience. It may also refer to the role of the leader in reflecting problem solving (pp. 6–7). Torrington et al. (2005) further suggested that leadership is predominantly an inborn aptitude that cannot be accomplished basically through training, although it can be further improved through education. Grint (1991) agrees with this view, noting 'it would be odd if leadership was the only human skill that could not be enhanced through understanding and practice (p. 2)'.

Leadership could also be further understood by considering how top management develop their previous experience and expertise to clarify the ideas of followers and encourage creativity (Berson et al. 2006; Mumford et al. 2003). As such, leadership may be seen as part of a learning process succeeding through carrying out day-to-day responsibilities. Logically, this may be mediated through individual experience and learning preference.

Arguably, leadership is a key factor in creating organisational learning. This could be accomplished by building a sense of commitment among members of the organisation based on a shared vision. Furthermore, Daft (2000) recommended that leadership is significant in organisations aiming to transform themselves into learning organisations. It is important to note, however, that different styles of leadership may develop different ways of encouraging employees (Bass 1985). Similarly, William et al. (1993) recognised that although everyone has the potential to be a leader, there is no single style or personality that is best for all situations. Likewise, there are neither correct nor incorrect ways of leading; effective leadership styles must be appropriate to any organisation seeking for improved organisational performance (Bush and Glover 2012). Nevertheless, regardless of which styles are adopted, it is widely accepted that leadership is an indispensable perspective which top management need to understand to promote a learning environment.

Kotter (2008) demonstrated that the single most important factor in successful organisational change is knowledgeable leadership. Leaders or top management provide the highest leverage point for changes to arise because they are critical to establishing the strategic direction of the organisation as well as in creating and maintaining its culture (Sidle 2005; Kotter 2008). More importantly, scholars have emphasised that leadership and performance are two important and interrelated variables contributing to organisational performance, and thus there is a critical need to examine this relationship (see, for example, Hadikin and O'Driscoll 2000; Tepper 2000). It appears that leadership is an important ideal for top management in their role to encourage learning, share knowledge with and transfer it to employees by means of appropriate styles in different situations for the purpose of achieving organisational goals.

It has been suggested that the transformational leadership approach is more effective than others in creating change in an organisation, especially compared with transactional leadership. This has also been related to the way to lower the barriers to transferring knowledge within the organisation (see, for example, Easterby-Smith and Lyles 2011). In the recent literature, Bass and Avolio are widely acknowledged for continuing these new leadership concepts. In line with Bryman (1999, p. 31), their basic ideas are greatly influenced by Burn's (1978) work. Burn recommended that transactional leadership is more common than is transformational leadership, if less dramatic in its consequences. Bass (1997), however, further developed the concepts of transactional and transformational leadership. He established them as two separate theories and distinguished their different features (Judge and Piccolo 2004).

Bass (1997) proposed that transformational leaders are expected to make their employees trust, respect and appreciate them by concentrating on idealised influence, individualised consideration and inspirational motivation, which in turn implies serving as a charismatic role model and expressing a vision that could be created. It also suggests a need for intellectual stimulation, defined as questioning old assumptions and the status quo (Avolio and Bass 1995). This leadership style describes top management likely to concentrate on higher motivation development, encouraging subordinates' motivation by an inspiring vision of the future (Rowold and Heinitz 2007; Bass 1997).

Similarly, Yukl (1999) argues that charismatic leadership and transformational leadership are partially overlapping concepts. Hence, it is suggested that transformational leadership could be considered to be the concept that comprehensively covers charismatic leadership, visionary leadership and cultural leadership (Kuhert 1994). It also explains the process of leadership that is able to influence people in the organisation in both specific and general areas. To support this, Alves et al. (2007) proposed that a continuous learning culture is expedient for any organisation seeking improved performance. In particular, Martins and Terblanche (2003) suggested that top management is required to encourage curiosity in organisational members, to ascertain new knowledge and valuable solutions to be introduced into the workplace. To sum up, it describes top management who emphasise building employees' motivation to generate productivity for the entire organisation.

Elaborating further, transformational leadership theory could be considered a form of behavioural theory. It is based on the premise that leadership can be learned (Hetland and Sandal 2003; Bass 1997). More importantly, there is substantial evidence suggesting that transformational leadership helps to increase higher levels of individual performance (Avolio and Bass 1995; Avolio and Yammarino 2013). For example, Hater and Bass (1988) and Ilies et al. (2006) concluded that top management at Federal Express who were evaluated as transformational leaders attained better performance. However, Yukl (1999) argued that Bass and Avolio's leadership theory can be strengthened through the indispensable impact of developments identified more clearly and used to explain how each type of behaviour affects each type of mediating variable and outcome.

Arguably, as the preceding discussion suggests, transformational leaders are often characterised as organisational champions managing improvements, initiating innovative ideas and motivating organisational members. Through their personal charisma, these individuals inspire trust, faith and belief in themselves, their vision and their actions. Yet while the virtues of these charismatic leaders are frequently praised in the popular management press, there can be drawbacks with such forms of leadership.

Howell and Avolio (1993) believed that this type of leader can become so fascinated by their vision of what is best for the organisation, that they unintentionally neglect internal and external signals that their vision might not be appropriate. Numerous cautionary tales exist where top management were so carried away with their personal vision that they literally destroyed their organisations in the process. Another criticism is that this type of top management does not necessarily act in the best interests of their organisation. Many employ their power to restructure their companies in their own image. They often entirely blur the boundary separating their personal interests from their organisation's interests. At its worst, the risks of this ego-driven charisma are top management enabling their self-interest and personal goals to dominate the goals of the organisation. Similarly, these top management occasionally surround themselves with organisational members terrified to share their attitudes, so when the top management make any mistake, the organisational members do not oppose the management's ideas (Seltzer and Bass 1990).

Compared to the transformational leadership approach, transactional leadership is largely acknowledged as the traditional management function of leading (Daft 2007; Bass 1997). There are three key dimensions making up transactional leadership, namely contingent rewards, management by exception-active and management by exception-passive. Contingent rewards refer to the degree to which the leader sets up constructive transactions or exchanges with subordinates. Transactional leadership clarifies expectations and establishes the rewards for reaching these expectations. In contrast, management by exception-active refers to top management monitoring organisational members' behaviour, anticipating problems and taking corrective action before the behaviour creates serious difficulties. On the other hand, management by exception-passive means top management taking action only after the behaviours of the organisational members have already created difficulties (Judge and Piccolo 2004).

It is noted that top managements who have this leadership style prefer to provide appropriate rewards, focus on clarifying the role and task requirements of organisational members, and initiate structure (Kuhert 1994). These attributes of transactional leadership could lead to an increase in organisational performance as researchers have suggested that managers with this leadership style tend to be hardworking. They are more concerned with the accomplishment of the assigned tasks than the development of organisational members' capabilities (Daft 2000). These two different leadership styles may both be present, but this does not mean they are equally important. Hence, Bass (1997) and Seltzer and Bass (1990) proposed that to accomplish improved organisational performance, a combination of transactional and transformational leaders is required. Nonetheless, some studies have found a mix of both positive and negative correlation between transactional leadership and performance (Gellis 2001; Howell and Avolio 1993).

In comparison to transformational and transactional leadership, laissez-faire describes top management who are neither task-concerned nor people-concerned. They avoid providing direction to the organisational members. They try not to make decisions, often hesitate in taking action and are not present when required. Laissez-faire leadership is also interconnected with management by exception-passive leadership (Judge and Piccolo 2004).

It appears that such managers are not highly driven; their power only comes from their position in the organisation and they are less likely to carry out their responsibilities. Almost inevitably, laissez-faire leadership is likely to result in damaging consequences for the working surroundings, health and well-being of organisational members (Corrigan et al. 2000; Hetland and Sandal 2003)

Thus far, several studies have scrutinised leadership style to find different practices to improve organisational performance. For example, in emphasising the prominence of the knowledge-based approach for research and development (R&D) teams, Kammerlind et al. (2004) and Shin and Jing (2007) also found that transformational leadership and educational specialisation heterogeneity interact with each other, contributing substantially to team creativity. They found that the two variables are statistically strongly associated with team creativity. More specifically, the teams' creative efficiency mediated the relationship between educational specialisation heterogeneity, transformational leadership and team creativity.

Similarly, Gellis (2001) studied the relationship between transactional and transformational leadership styles and their impact on performance. Totally, 187 employees were asked to rate multifactor leadership questionnaires. He found that transformational and transactional leadership styles are correlated with organisational performance.

The influences of transformational leadership on organisational performance were also investigated by Colbert et al. (2008). Totally, 94 top management teams were asked to participate. They found that top management transformational leadership was positively related to within-team goal importance congruence, which in turn was positively related to organisational performance. Similarly, Howell et al. (2005) predicted the relationship between leadership and organisational performance. 101 top managements were selected as their sample, and they found that transformational leadership is positively related to business performance, while contingent reward leadership was not significantly related to it.

Moreover, the findings also suggest that physical distance between top management and employees negatively mediated the relationship between transformational leadership and organisational performance, but positively mediated the relationship between contingent reward leadership and organisational performance. In addition, several studies have attempted to study the relationship between gender and leadership styles. They found that gender is significantly correlated with leadership styles, and that female top managements are likely to adopt more transformational leadership (Lantz 2008).

In contrast, Mandell and Pherwani (2003) and Oshagbemi (2008) proposed that although there were significant differences between gender and the leadership styles of top management they found that age is directly related to leadership styles of the top managements.

Leadership theory has also been applied in studies on human resource management and organisational performance. Weichun et al. (2005) studied the relationship between human resource management and leadership styles of the top managements, using 170 firms in Singapore as samples. They found that human resource management fully mediates the relationship between top managements' transformational leadership and subjective assessment of organisational performance. It also partially mediates the relationship between top managements' transformational leadership and absenteeism.

Mccall et al. (1988) emphasised the relationship between leadership and the factors influencing development as a top manager; the most positive impacts comprised job assignments the executive had experienced; critical circumstance they had gone through; relationships and interactions with others; and formal training and education. Similarly, Dalton et al. (1999) emphasised that 75 % of career events that top managements attribute to their successful development derived from a combination of learning from experience in taking responsibility for routine tasks, and learning from organisational members.

In addition, Noruzy et al. (2013) predicted the connection between leadership styles, organisational learning, knowledge management, organisational innovation and organisational performance. They found that transformational leadership positively and indirectly influenced organisational innovation through organisational learning and knowledge management. Knowledge management and organisational learning influenced organisational performance indirectly by organisational innovation. They also recommended that top management should consider applying a transformational role and the use of organisational learning and knowledge management; this would create organisational innovation and consequently enhance organisational performance. Correspondingly, Bryant (2003) asserted that transformational leadership could be more effective at creating and sharing knowledge at the individual and group levels, while transactional leadership is more practical at developing knowledge at the organisational level.

Similarly, Glastra et al. (2004) proposed that the organisation-created learning environment may support top management in developing the skills and reflexivity needed to handle the responsibilities necessary in today's business. Likewise, Salge et al. (2013) found that the relationship between knowledge management and leadership styles of top management could be helpful where there is an effective leadership style and helpful organisational environment for sustaining learning within the organisation.

PKM may thus facilitate top management in recognising how to adopt their experience to develop their leadership style. In turn, top management may be able to transfer knowledge and strengthen their organisation for future challenges and increasing competitive and innovative capabilities. Therefore, this may show that top managements' different approaches to individual learning may influence development of their leadership styles.

Wang and Poutziouris (2010) have scrutinised the relationship between leadership styles and organisational performance. They obtained complete data from a variety of sources for 5,710 SMEs in the UK. They found that there is a strong connection between the two variables and suggest that leadership training programmes provided by local government and development agencies are necessary for improving leadership skills for top management.

In a different context, Fred et al. (2005) studied the nature of the relationship between transformational leadership and two work-related attitudes, organisational commitment and job satisfaction. They compared Kenya and the United States, obtaining a response rate of 82% from Kenya and 86% from the USA (158 and 189 respondents, respectively). They concluded that transformational leadership has a strong and positive significant association with organisational commitment and job satisfaction in both cultures. Mirkamali et al. (2011) studied the connection between leadership style and organisational learning in commercial organisations, with 120 members of top management being asked to participate in the data collection. The results show a strong connection between learning and leadership, suggesting that positive and meaningful relations were revealed between the components of transformational leadership and organisational learning. In particular, idealised influence (behaviour) as one of the dimensions of transformational leadership is the most important predictor of organisational learning, as suggested by Longest et al. (1993). Also, they found that experience was not correlated with organisational learning, but gender and education are.

In terms of cultural differences, Hofstede (1993, p. 81) emphasised that 'there is no such thing as universal management theories'. Also, he explained the process of top management in the American sense that (1) top management apply skills to manage the organisation only, but do not own the business; and (2) top management create and motivate teamwork among organisational members. Top management carry a high status and many American men and women aspire to the role. In the US, the top manager is a cultural hero. Hofstede (1993, p. 86) also studied the effect of Chinese culture. Taiwan, Hong Kong and Singapore are composed of overseas Chinese with wealthy economic status, compared to those living in other parts of Asia. Overseas Chinese also play a very important role in the economies of Indonesia, Malaysia, the Philippines and Thailand, where they form an ethnic minority. Hofstede (1993) asserted that these overseas Chinese firms rely on networking in certain areas they are familiar with; these networks are built on trust among Chinese firms' members. They are family-owned, and most of the decision-making is in the hands of one dominant family member. They are likely to keep a low profile. This shows that the diversity in management accepted in one nation may not be recognised in another, due to the difference in culture (Gathers 2003). Similarly, the most appropriate form of management may vary between countries. Based on Hofstede's work (1993, p. 86) the culture of overseas Chinese may also influence the style of top management in Thailand, in managing their firms differently, such as their focus on one product and market, and relying on personal trust to build up a network.

In addition, even though effective leadership is widely seen as desirable, in some cultures this is not the case. The study by House et al. (2004) into the relationship between the effectiveness of leadership and different cultures looked at six culturally implicit theories of leadership: Charismatic/Value-based, team-oriented, participative, autonomous, humane and self-protective. In most cultures, the first of these is considered most desirable. The second is desirable. The other leadership styles, except for self-protective, are seen as acceptable. But whereas the first is universally desirable, the other patterns are often culturally contingent. To be ambitious, for instance, is 'appropriate' in some cultures and 'inappropriate' in others. They also found that performance orientation is related to all culturally implied theories of leadership, except for self-protective. Self-protective leadership focuses on ensuring the safety and security of the individual and group through status enhancement and face saving. This leadership dimension includes five sub-scales labelled (a) self-centred, (b) status conscious, (c) conflict inducer, (d) face saver and (e) procedural. Furthermore, self-protective leadership is linked especially to charismatic leadership.

However, House and colleagues (2004) found that the respondents in Thailand attained the highest rate of self-protective, which is closely linked to the Charismatic/Value-based leadership. This may imply that different patterns of leadership style may be perceived as good patterns dependent on cultural factors. In particular, House et al. (2004) proposed that Thailand is a developing country, the majority of whose people are Buddhist. They also suggested that in developing countries, particularly in the rural areas, the normal way of life is such that children take care of their parents and provide material help in their old age. The social norms help create culture. It is possible that Thailand as a Buddhist country reflects a diversity of cultures.

Fundamentally, followers of this religion are encouraged to progress from becoming more compassionate to becoming more generous, to detaching themselves from worldly desires, to becoming more focused mentally on spiritual wisdom and purity (House et al. 2004). Hence, it may be possible that the religion of Thailand has developed a culture in which Thais are likely to be generous and normally look after their parents in their old age. So, the findings showed that the Thai respondents attaining the highest rate of self-protective, closely related to Charismatic/Value-based leadership, are likely to inspire, to motivate and to anticipate high-performance outcomes, and are relatively committed to the teaching of Buddhism, which encourages people to be kind to others.

Related to its culture, House et al. (2004) also found that Thailand scores highest on the Future Orientation value scale, defined as the degree to which individuals in organisations or societies engage in future-oriented behaviours such as planning, investing in the future and delaying individual or collective gratification. They proposed that this may be because Thailand has a distinct emphasis on Buddhism.

In contrast, they found that the industrialised or developed countries with higher income populations attained a lower score on the Future Orientation value scale. They explained that the higher income nations may prefer to appreciate the present more because they have already accumulated substantial wealth and material resources. The lower income nations may see a stronger need for taking a long-term perspective and sacrificing for the future because they must contend with limited resources. Also, the effective leadership is closely connected to transactional leadership in which top management have almost absolute power to manipulate the organisation. Effective top management is expected to have a greater knowledge than his or her organisational members. Although the organisational members may have questions or feedback, this may be interpreted as impolite or disloyal (Holloway 2012; Hellriegel and Slocum 2011). This shows that culture may influence the perception of Thais to have different concepts from others.

To conclude, Bass and Avolio's approach is arguably one of the most prominent leadership theories in contemporary research. It provides much insight into how to create, change and sustain organisational learning (Avolio and Bass 1995; Brown and Keeping 2005; Judge and Bono 2000; Gleue 2002; Shin and Zhou 2007).

Although a number of scholars have declared that leadership is positively related to organisational performance, the interplay between leadership and diversity remains largely unexplored (Jackson et al. 2003; Kristy et al. 2007), suggesting that the demographics of top management need to be studied, as well as leadership and PKM. Bass (1997) and Seltzer and Bass (1990) pointed out that transactional and transformational leadership should not be viewed separately. Both relate to how to inspire employees and increase organisational performance, including consideration of individuals, intellectual stimulation, inspirational motivation and idealised influence, as well as how top management can provide rewards appropriately. Hence, top management who practise both transactional and transformational leadership may increase the level of organisational performance.

Nonetheless, based on Hofstede's (1993) belief that 'there is no such thing as universal management theories', not only did House et al. (2004) say that Thailand is a developing country most of whose population is Buddhist; Hofstede (1993) also asserted that Thailand is influenced by the overseas Chinese culture, in which top management may develop different approaches to achieving organisational goals, such as focusing on cost cutting or pricing strategies. So, it is possible that with different cultures, top management may develop different ways to improve organisational performance. To a large extent, the leadership style supportive to a particular business is in need of further investigation. Taking into account the various strengths and limitations of previous research into leadership styles, this study attempts to incorporate Bass and Avolio's leadership theory specifically, and to study its relationship to organisational performance.

2.1.10 Organisational Performance

For decades, the term 'organisational performance' has been defined from a wide range of perspectives; some scholars distinguish it as multi-dimensional, proposing that each organisation has particular criteria for organisational performance, and the criteria applicable in one organisation may not be appropriate in others (Grünberg 2004; Lumpkin and Dess 2001). The organisational performance factors identified in specific cases are associated with individual local cases and purposes. Hence, it is essential for the fundamental components of organisational performance to be appropriately characterised (Grünberg 2004). Nonetheless, scholars have developed a definition of organisational performance and criteria pertinent across organisations and meaningfully located within a general theoretical arrangement (Bandura 2000; Bolino and Turnley 2003; Chan 2009; Hornaday and Wheatley 1986). Traditional analysts emphasise that organisational performance for small business ventures embraces explanations of why people start their ventures, what problems business ownership overcomes and generates for the owners or top management, and specifically what the firm's top management actually desire to achieve for themselves (Beaver and Jennings 2001; Chaganti and Chaganti 1983; Marlow and Patton 1993; Thorpe 1989; Storey et al. 1987).

Recently, researchers have emphasised that understanding organisational performance can help to distinguish techniques for improvement (Halachmi 2005; Dess and Robinson 1984). Academic researchers have described organisational performance as an umbrella term for all concepts that consider the success of a company and its activities. Different organisations have different purposes in running their business; therefore, the determined goals of each organisation may be different and the levels of organisational performance may be varied (Fan et al. 2014). Organisational performance could be defined as the ability to reach a desired objective or the degree to which anticipated results are achieved (Stefan 2005). It could also be well-defined multi-dimensionally by looking at four different categories: achieving organisational goals, increasing resourcefulness, satisfying customers and improving internal processes (Cameron 1986; Redshaw 2001). Organisational performance also serves the purpose of monitoring performance, identifying the areas that require attention, enhancing motivation, improving communications and strengthening accountability (Waggoner et al. 1999). Amaratunga and Baldry (2002) defined organisational performance as a concept to help an organisation to set agreed-upon goals, allocate and prioritise resources, inform top management to either confirm or change policy or programme directions to achieve those goals, and share results of performance in pursuing those goals.

Furthermore, organisational performance can refer to the level of productivity that the organisation can accomplish towards attaining its goals, increasing organisational resources, meeting customers' needs and improving internal processes. Scholars have proposed that the organisation's resources are the source of sustainable competitive advantages to support the organisation in improving performance (Dierickx and Cool 1989; Afiouni 2007). These resources must be rare, valuable, without substitutes and difficult to imitate (Alvarez and Barney 2002; Markides and Williamson 1996). In order to sustain organisational competitiveness and success, organisational learning concepts have been offered to facilitate and enhance levels of productivity (Paparoidamis 2005; Dunphy et al. 1996; Ghobadian and O'Regan 2006).

Simultaneously, evidence shows that organisational performance is used to determine organisational learning in different areas (see, for example, Murray 2003; Panayides 2007; Pemberton et al. 2001; Spicer and Sadler-Smith 2006; Vakola and Rezgui 2000; Vincent and Ross 2001). Similarly, a variety of approaches to evaluating organisational performance have been applied to help continue learning in the organisation (see, for example, Afiouni 2007; Aragon-Correa et al. 2007; Chang and Lee 2007; Michie and Sheehan-Quinn 2001; Michie and Zumitzavan 2012). Marr (2006) recommended that it is important to create a learning environment in the organisation in order to heighten organisational performance. Kaplan and Norton (1998) proposed that there is a close connection between organisational learning and organisational performance; in order to embolden the learning environment in the organisation, the top manager is the key person encouraging this to take place.

In more detail, Marr (2006) said that it is essential that not only do top management need to participate in supporting a learning environment but also all organisation members. To do so, he suggested that the organisation needs to encourage organisational learning through a social context in which members can share knowledge both tacitly and explicitly, and encourage commitment, collaboration, mutual respect and a sense of belonging. Specifically, every organisational member needs to feel important to the community and integrated to create value as a whole. In an even more complex example from the service business sector, Singapore Airlines has encouraged all of its staff to share and relocate knowledge jointly. This leads to the development of an 'organisational identity', so that all members feel that they are important to the organisation and are fully willing to serve customers to the best of their ability (Chong 2007). To encourage learning in the organisation, Singapore Airlines provided training from the lowest to the top positions of the organisation. Eventually, as in the healthcare industry, Liu et al. (2006) and Rusnakova et al. (2004) established that customer satisfactions had been raised and, in turn, organisational performance had been improved.

Researchers generally view organisational performance by two main measures: Objective and subjective. For example, Waybright and Kemp (2012) compared objective measures to the scores of league sports; financial statements help the scorekeepers, or accountants, to collect financial data about how well the organisation has scored; data such as sales volumes, profits or return on assets is taken from financial records and externally recorded and audited accounts. Against this solid evidence which determines which team wins, there are subjective measures as reported by respondents themselves (Wall et al. 2004).

Several studies have considered the relationship between different management concepts and organisational performance in the form of objective measures (Zahra et al. 2007b). For example, Tower et al. (2007) studied relationships in the small business sector between family businesses and organisational performance, concentrating on financial performance. A sample of 241 small firms was surveyed. There were significant differences in the planning processes between businesses that held family meetings and those that did not. No differences were found in the performance measures. Significant relationships between family meetings and both planning processes and performance measures were found. In addition, Carlson et al. (2006) analysed a sample of 168 family-owned fast-growth small and medium enterprises to empirically examine the consequences of five human resource practices on sales-growth performance. They found that training and development, a recruitment package, maintaining morale, use of performance appraisals and competitive compensation were more important for high sales-growth performing firms than for low sales-growth performing firms (Carlson et al. 2006).

Furthermore, Pett and Wolff (2007) explored the connection between product improvement and organisational performance based on the growth of the organisation as one dimension and profitability as another. Their sample of 855 small- and medium-sized organisations was randomly selected. They found that the product improvement orientation was positively related to growth and financial performance, that is profitability, but the process improvement orientation showed no statistical relationship to growth or ultimately to profitability.

On the other hand, subjective measures of organisational performance (Garg et al. 2003) are cost-effective because data can be collected through questionnaires or interview surveys that simultaneously obtain information on practices. In smaller organisations there may be few appreciable financial records, and even for those organisations which do keep such records, the data may not be held in an appropriate form compatible with the required level of analysis. In general, subjective measures tend to involve questioning respondents to evaluate their company's performance against their competitors' (Wall et al. 2004).

Subjective measures have been widely used to measure organisational performance in the service sector, and in particular in the healthcare industry (Ramasamy et al. 2007; Patton et al. 2000; Sahay 2005). To elaborate, the data collected for measuring the levels of organisational performance must be interconnected with the dimension of the organisational goals so that the organisation can compare itself with competitors in the same business sector. Marr (2006) proposed that in measuring organisational performance, an organisation must focus on its specific goal. As an example, some organisations may rely on the number of calls from call centres to measure customer satisfaction. Similarly, a department store may rely on the number of people visiting per day, although some of these observed people may not be customers as they do not purchase any products from the store. Thus, to accurately measure organisational performance subjectively, appropriate data must be collected that is strongly related to organisational goals.

For example, the researchers have found that there is a close link between the balance scorecard (BSC) and the perception of organisational members, considered a subset of subjective measures to evaluate different levels of organisational performance. They found that the BSC can help the organisation to fill missing areas of organisational development, even though the BSC remains imperfect (Correa et al. 2014).

However, there is academic research from the Medical Group Practice Environment (Minnis and Elmuti 2008) which evaluates the relationship between objective and subjective measures by testing the correlation between financial performance and perceived performance. The statistical test indicates that there is no correlation between the two variables; however, the authors advised that different cultures, regions and business sectors may produce different results. To summarise, organisational performance can be measured objectively and subjectively. Objective measures rely on the complete record of company data whilst the subjective measures tend to ask respondents to appraise their organisational performance vis-à-vis their competitors. Thus, organisational performance can be determined by concentrating on different measurements, according to the goals of each organisation.

The nature of small business means that top management plays a vital role in establishing and developing the organisation; however, the relentless drive for personal achievement may reduce growth potential and ultimately may threaten the survival of the organisation (Bellas 2004). The top manager is the key person in the organisation who clarifies the organisational goals and in turn drives the level of success in the organisation. In order to accomplish the organisational goals, the top management needs to understand and explain organisational performance, which could then help in piloting the organisation to achieve its goals. Several researchers have suggested approaches to improving the organisation, through good management to accomplish effectiveness, so understanding organisational performance could support the top management to run the company more effectively at different levels.

In addition, Pett and Wolff (2007) recommended that organisations in the same environment but of different sizes may create different levels of organisational performance. A variety of academic researchers found both negative and positive correlations between the number of employees and organisational performance. Arocena et al. (2007) investigated the relationship between gender and financial performance in 160 small accounting practices. The findings suggest that although financial performance appears to be significantly different for female-owned and male-owned organisations, these performance differences are explained by several variables other than gender directly.

Similarly, Wiersema and Bantel (1992) studied the relationship between the demographics of top management and organisational performance in American companies. They found an important association between the demographics and corporate strategic change, in turn improving organisational performance. They found that younger top management with less experience and higher levels of education contributed to generating higher levels of performance. Correspondingly, Al-Ahmadi (2009) investigated the relationship between the demographics of top management and organisational performance in a hospital in Saudi Arabia. The results indicated that job performance is positively related to some personal factors, including years of experience, nationality, gender and marital status. Level of education is negatively related to performance. Experience, nationality and marital status are significantly correlated with organisational performance, but level of education has a negative correlation.

Kotey and Folker (2007) supposed that education, type of employment or industry, and other types of experience help to prepare top managements for the challenges of business competition and to transfer their knowledge, skill and experience to employees; these are related to organisational performance. Shrader and Siegel (2007) studied the relationship between key attributes of top management and organisational performance. They applied longitudinal studies to investigate 198 high-tech organisations and found characteristics that are significantly related to organisational performance. In particular, technical experience has a direct association with organisational performance (Shrader and Siegel 2007). So, it appears that the top management of a small firm is the one who is most appropriate to evaluate its organisational performance.

Hodges and Kent (2006) scrutinised the relationship between planning sophistication and organisational performance. This research took a different approach by using a one-on-one interview technique with closed questions to evaluate management perceptions of planning sophistication and its relationship to perceptions of organisational performance. The results show that top management's perceptions of greater sophistication in their planning efforts are slightly positively related to perceptions of better organisational performance. They emphasised that increased knowledge would have some impact on an organisation's future performance.

2.2 The Link Between Personal Knowledge Management, Leadership Styles and Organisational Performance

Smith and Kolb (1996) argue that people learn through their experience, and that the role of experience is important in shaping the process of learning. Relating this to the leadership style of top management, Kouzes and Posner (1995) argue that role experience is powerfully associated with the manner in which top management acquire leadership skills. This suggests that the role of experience would allow top management to effectively learn from their own experience and the experience of others (O'Sullivan 1999). Brown and Posner (2001) found that how people learn is significantly associated with how they act as top managers. The results also specified that top managers who frequently engaged in PKM also employed a greater variety of leadership styles, such as challenging, inspiring, enabling, modelling and encouraging. PKM and transformational leadership style are significantly correlated.

Marquardt and Waddill (2004) also asserted that what top management learn and how they learn cannot be separated, because how individuals learn influences what they learn. This suggests that PKM which enables individuals to understand how they learn may help them to learn more successfully. Ellinger et al. (2002) discovered that most organisational members learned in an informal manner. Furthermore, Fox (1997) proposed that much of what is learned by top management is learned informally.

On the other hand, Mccall et al. (1988) found that the factors that impact on the development of leadership are job assignments experienced by top management, critical situations they had gone through, relationships and interactions with others and formal training and education. Posner (2009) also proposed that people learn from their experience, whether formal or informal, structured or naturally occurring. This indicates that while top management may learn through their experience, PKM has a positive correlation with leadership styles, and may help them to apply and learn more effectively through their experience (Jones 2013).

In addition, researchers in multidisciplinary areas revealed that PKM influences the development of skills and attitudes, initiating more effective cognition, communication, collaboration, creativity, problem solving, lifelong learning, social networking, leadership and the like (Doyle 2014). These approaches raise PKM to a more sophisticated level than information management, and can help individuals acquire useful knowledge and organise it into a perspective enabling more effective decision-making in their day-to-day responsibilities (Zuber-Skerritt 2005; Durand and Dorsey 2000; Jefferson 2006).

However, Dawson and Andriopoulos (2014) argue that it is important to note that under different forms of organisational structure, management style, organisational culture and business sector, different organisations may acquire different levels of organisational performance. They claimed that it may be significant that even though some organisations have skilful top management, the level of success may be varied because some but not all of top management directly organise the firm. Hence, the levels of transition knowledge in different organisations may be varied, and this may influence the level of organisational performance. Further, even though transformational leadership is known as the appropriate style of leadership for top management who are seeking to transfer and encourage knowledge within the organisation, there are other influencing variables since the process involves different experiences, styles of perceiving information or notions of the top management and organisational members. Faust (1984) said that 'scientists may have sufficient cognitive ability to comprehend relationship among variables, but insufficient ability to comprehend more complex relationships'.

If nature revealed everything to us, how much would we be able to understand? Similarly, to what extent can the differences in experience, educational levels, PKM and leadership styles of top management transfer and knowledge to organisational members and how can these influences be linked to organisational performance? In turn, can they be related to how much organisational members perceive and interpret the notions they implement in their day-to-day responsibilities, ultimately enhancing overall organisational performance?

According to Posner (2009), individuals capable of understanding different circumstances and developing in different situations would have an advantage in learning how to lead and potentially become the best top management. This happens because they are better able to appreciate a variety of situations than those more narrowly focused or limited in their methodology for learning, and hence are more successful leaders. Posner (2009) also suggested that leadership development is a learning process in itself. Hence, PKM can help individuals seeking to understand how to learn effectively; they may utilise their leadership style to manage their organisation under any circumstances.

Justifiably, the determined development of top managements has a positive influence on organisational performance (Mabey and Ramirez 2005). Top management who know how to learn and utilise their leadership effectively would be able to make use of the unique capabilities of their employees through HRM practices. In the long term, this would enhance organisational performance.

2.3 Conclusion

This chapter has surveyed the literatures related to the notion of PKM, leadership styles and organisational performance, and has pointed to the connection between these concepts, which is the focus of our research reported in this book. The following chapter discusses the quantitative methods we applied for this research.

Chapter 3
Research Methodology

3.1 Introduction

Chapter 1 indicated the study's research objectives; the current chapter explains how our data were collected, and discusses the quantitative research methods which we applied. This is followed by a detailed explanation of the procedures we applied, and lastly questions regarding the reliability and validity of such methods are discussed.

3.1.1 Methodological Issues

In a highly competitive, globalised business world, new problems and issues emerge demanding innovation and flexibility. The philosophy of social science is to attempt to establish connections with the everyday experience of those being studied, and to ensure that the results of social scientific research are made accessible to a wide audience. Scientific or objective knowledge can be taken as a true account of something, and scientific explanations can be applied universally. This is particularly true when knowledge is detached from specific experience in a single situation; in this specific substance, objective knowledge is reflected in the appearance of causal processes (Smith 1998, pp. 5, 27).

In the social sciences, knowledge can be acquired by both deduction and induction. While deduction tends to be related to an objective, quantitative approach, induction is likely to be correlated with the subjective or qualitative approach; appropriate methodologies are applied to answer specific research questions (Bryman 2006, p. 5). Gerring (2007) suggests that there are two ways to learn how to construct a house: by studying the construction of many houses, or the construction of a particular house. The first technique is called cross-case, and the latter is a case study. Although they are different, they are mutually dependent. Cross-case study naturally provides a broader view to understanding the

© The Author(s) 2015
V. Zumitzavan and J. Michie, *Personal Knowledge Management, Leadership Styles, and Organisational Performance*, SpringerBriefs in Business,
DOI 10.1007/978-981-287-438-2_3

significance of any subject. In contrast, a case study provides more insight by intensively studying the individual substance. It is difficult to imagine cross-case research that does not draw upon case study work, or case study work that discards adjacent cases. They are unique, but synergistic tools in the analysis of social life.

To a large extent, cross-case analysis is more appropriate in the quantitative technique. Morse (1991) and Gerring (2007) asserted that a cross-case study generally requires a large sample consisting of multiple cases which can be analysed statistically. The central philosophy of the quantitative approach is that everything in the universe can be described numerically (McQueen and Knussen 2002).

According to Saunders et al. (2009) 'to pursue the principle of scientific rigour the deductive approach dictates that the researchers should be independent of what is being observed'. Hence, a number of samples were collected and analysed formally in the quantitative phase: number of employees, age, gender, educational levels and the lengths of management experience, need to be recorded in a way that enables events to be measured quantitatively (Saunders et al. 2009). Similarly, the leadership styles of top management who have different demographic backgrounds may also vary and may lead to different levels of organisational performance. Furthermore, the researchers realise that this analysis is implicitly related to the specificities of business situations; therefore, this research requires an understanding of the meanings humans attach to events, such as the perspective of top management in terms of managing their organisations.

The nature of the quantitative approach helps to explain relationships among the variables investigated. This approach is employed to scrutinise the main objectives of this research, i.e. to identify the characteristics of top management of the hospitals and explore their relationships to the success of the organisation through a consideration of PKM and leadership style theories (Hancock 2006). From studying these patterns and relationships, hypotheses have been developed to test the relationships between top managements' demographics, PKM, leadership style and organisational performance. The quantitative data collected to test these hypotheses is subjected to descriptive statistics, correlation and multiple regression analysis.

In conclusion, cross-cases were applied to collect the survey questionnaires, categorised into the quantitative approach to answer the research questions.

3.1.2 Research Methods and Designs

This section summarises how this research endeavours to answer the research questions. More specifically, it provides an overview of the research field and establishes the characteristics of top management.

The compatibility of quantitative data and the use of primary and secondary data are also noted by the researchers, and data from previous academic research was used as a guideline. The results from the questionnaire were analysed using the Statistics Package for Social Science program (SPSS). Additionally, secondary data has been used to represent the overall image of the healthcare industry. Thus, the researchers aim to contrive a quantitative approach to apply to the empirical questions of this research with the purpose of ensuring that the data collected is practical.

In social science research, the survey strategy is one of the most useful methods to apply in order to draw general conclusions, if the samples have been selected appropriately. Generally, survey research concerns the opinions, attitudes, motives, values and norms of the research units. The survey method is most commonly associated with the written questionnaire (van der Velde et al. 2008). In this research, as part of the deductive approach, the survey technique was used as a tool to collect empirical data from the respondents. It is thus essential that the unit of analysis needs to be identified in conjunction with the primary and secondary data that need to be categorised beforehand in order to select useful information related to the research topic for the data analysis (Balnaves and Caputi 2001).

3.1.3 Unit of Analysis

In order to draw an appropriate sample from which results can be generalised, it is essential that the unit of analysis be identified and be appropriate in terms of the research objectives (Balnaves and Caputi 2001; van der Velde et al. 2008). According to Saunders et al. (2009), 'the majority of top management are familiar with the deductive approach so that those top management or policy-makers are likely to put faith in the conclusions stemming from this approach'. Therefore, hospital's top management is chosen as the unit of analysis in this research.

3.1.4 Primary Data

The questionnaire is one of the most widely used survey data-collection techniques. It refers to all techniques of data collection in which individuals are requested to answer the same set of questions in a prearranged order (de Vaus 2002). There are several strengths of conducting a questionnaire. It provides a comparatively effortless and direct approach to the study's attitudes, values, beliefs and motives (Robson 2002), and it is relatively efficient in terms of time and cost. It is apposite for both descriptive questions and testing hypotheses (May 2011). However, there are some weaknesses: it depends on the readiness and the ability of respondents to answer the questionnaire (van der Velde et al. 2008). Robson (2002) suggested that 'what they say might contradict what they have done and they will not necessary report their real attitudes', in which case the respondents may offer partial or biased answers and the result may not be accurate. Therefore, the researchers asked respondents whether they were willing to participate in the research, and triangulated the combined primary and secondary data to enhance the reliability and validity.

3.1.5 Secondary Data

Saunders et al. (2009) discuss how secondary data can be divided into three main sub-categories: documentary, survey-based data and those compiled from multiple sources. Unquestionably, documentary data plays a vital role in this research. There are books, journal and newspaper articles, surveys and publicly available official statistics of the Thai government; several sources are available through the Internet. Different types of documentary data have also been used to strengthen the analysis of the research questions and meet the research objectives.

The main advantage of using secondary data is the saving of resources such as time and money; it is readily accessible, relatively inexpensive and quickly obtained (Ghauri and Grønhaug 2005). Saunders et al. (2009) stated that 'if you need your data quickly, secondary data may be the only viable alternative'. The savings give the researchers more time to think about theoretical aims and substantive issues.

Nevertheless, there are some disadvantages, for example, gaining access to the data may be difficult or costly. Saunders et al. (2009) suggested that there are a range of available online indexes with direct links to downloadable files, but such sources may not be valid or reliable. Therefore, the secondary data used in this research was carefully selected.

Ideally, the distinct advantages of a quantitative approach would reduce bias and help to understand the environment of the healthcare industry (Ragin 1989). In this research, the survey was conducted with different top managers, to understand the correlation among their demographics, PKM and leadership styles, towards organisational performance. In a nutshell, the quantitative approach is likely to be more time saving. Specifically, selecting top management of hospitals within the same industry as the unit of analysis ensures that they have the same levels of understanding and backgrounds, and the nature of their position permits them to cope with different situations in the business. Therefore, the quantitative approach has been applied to study the behaviour and attitudes of top management as the unit of analysis.

3.2 Quantitative Approach

3.2.1 Attitude Scale

Attitude scales play an important role within questionnaire design; they are composed of a set of statements, and the respondents are asked to agree or disagree with the pre-coded answers. It is then possible to test a series of attitudes around a particular topic, rather than relying upon a single question as the indicator of a possibly complex set of attitudes (Oppenheim 1992). In this research, the Likert scale was applied in placing respondents' answers on an attitude continuum. Likert

(1932) is the most common form of multiple-item scales, permitting agreement or disagreement on individual items. Nonetheless, error or bias may arise if respondents avoid selecting the extreme response categories, or underestimate or overestimate the qualities of people or things they dislike or like. Balnaves and Caputi (2001) suggested that it is therefore essential to test the validity and reliability of items in scales. One of the most popular ways to ensure internal consistency is Cronbach's alpha coefficient (Saunders et al. 2009) explaining inter-relationships among the various items used to measure respondents' underlying attitudes. Cronbach's alpha ranges from 0 to 1: the closer to 1 indicates higher reliability and the minimum value accepted should ensure a reliability of 0.7 (Auamnoy 2002; Bryman and Cramer 2001; Pallant 2010).

3.2.2 Pilot Study

The purpose of the pilot study is to increase the clarity of the questionnaire so that respondents will not have difficulties in understanding and answering questions. It also provides a better understanding of the frames of reference relevant to the questionnaire and question wording. It may also help test the validity and reliability of the data collected (Balnaves and Caputi 2001; Saunders et al. 2009). Fink (1995) proposed that the minimum number of subjects for a pilot study is ten, which is adequate for a large survey of 100–200 responses (Dillman 2011). In fact, 30 sets of the pilot questionnaire were distributed in November 2012 to the top management and directors of hospitals in Thailand.

As a result, some of the respondents suggested different ways of structuring the question to be more specific, and some of these suggestions were implemented. For example, questions on age could ask for specific date of birth instead of the age in years. This was also emphasised by May (2011).

In addition, classification questions in the 'personal' section of the questionnaire, often referred to as demographics, might cause some discomfort (May 2011). In the pilot study they were located at the beginning of the questionnaire, but were relocated to the last section.

3.2.3 Sample

According to the Ministry of Public Health of Thailand (MOPH)'s statistical data in 2006, the population of this research interest is 1,468 hospitals throughout Thailand. Samples were classified by the Stratified Random Sampling method, ensuring that they were equitably selected with different locations in various provinces. Prior to conducting the questionnaire, postal letters, emails and telephone calls were made to arrange the time and to ascertain that the personnel were willing to participate in the survey. Respondents were assured of the confidentiality of their answers.

Krejcie and Morgan's (1970) formula for determining sample size shows that for a population size of 1,500 a sample size of no less than 306 is recommended (see Table A-22, Appendices). With a total number of 1,468 registered organisations, and allowing for an anticipated response rate of 11–15 % (Ames 2003), questionnaires were sent out to 1,000 of these organisations. However, a total of 539 completed questionnaires were received (a response rate of 53.9 %), which is good and should therefore give confidence as regards the validity of the research results and the generalisability of the findings. (Hair et al. (2010) suggest that, taking into account all the independent variables, a sample that is at least one-fifth of the target population size is required.)

To ensure reliability and validity, the pilot study was carried out before conducting the actual questionnaire survey. The questionnaire has four sections: demographics, PKM, leadership styles and organisational performance. The first section comprised questions relating to gender, age, education and experience, and the number of employees as a controlled variable. The second and third sections used a 1–6 Likert scale (Auamnoy 2002) where 1 indicated least and 6 most agreement with the statement supplied. In the last section, top management were asked to evaluate their organisation's performance by focusing on financial performance to provide a percentage score against other organisations in their sector.

3.2.4 Data Collection

The data collection took place from December 2012 to January 2013. Prior to conducting the questionnaires, the researchers had contacted the respondents to ask for participation and to notify them that their answers would be confidential and the content of the questionnaires used for academic purposes only. May (2011) suggests three main ways of conducting questionnaires: (1) Mail or self-completion questionnaire, (2) Telephone survey, (3) Face-to-face interview schedule. The first is a relatively cheap method of data collection, but the response rate is likely to be low. In order to increase the response rate, reminders and telephone calls were made two to four weeks after posting the initial questionnaire, and envelopes and stamps were provided for return. Telephone surveys are convenient and relatively cheap, and also offer faster collection; to ensure the number of returns and save time and money, a telephone survey was used simultaneously with the mail method. A face-to-face interview schedule is time-consuming, but it offers a clear, standardised and concise way to record the answers in accordance with the survey instructions, and maintains a rapport with the respondents (Fowler 2009). To ensure that questionnaires were delivered safely to as many respondents as possible within the time limitation, the researchers arranged to hand them to some respondents in person.

3.2.5 Reliability

Reliability refers to the stability, accuracy and dependability of the data (Burns 2000). Also, a valid question will enable accurate data to be collected, and one that is reliable will mean that the data is collected consistently (Saunders et al. 2009). Foddy (1994) recommends that 'the question must be understood by the respondents in the way intended by the researchers and the answer given by the respondents must be understood by the researchers in the way intended by the respondents'. Saunders et al. (2009) suggest that 'internal consistency' involves correlating the responses to each question with answers to other questions in the questionnaire. It therefore measures the consistency of responses across all or a subgroup of the questions. To ensure the reliability of the questionnaire, Cronbach's alpha was applied to test the internal consistency of each question in both the PKM and leadership style sections (see Table A-2 to A-21 in Appendices). Auamnoy (2002) and Pallant (2010) suggest that Cronbach's alpha should not be less than 0.70 or 49 % so that each construct could be related from one item to another. In this research, the PKM and leadership styles are greater than 0.70.

3.2.6 Validity

Balnaves and Caputi (2001) propose three main kinds of validity: construct, internal and external validity. Construct validity determines whether the construct of the research is successfully operationalised and represents the phenomena relating to the research objective. In this research, the unit of analysis is the top management of the healthcare industry, qualified to provide accurate data based on their knowledge.

Internal validity refers to the extent to which the research design really allows the researchers to draw conclusions about the relationships among variables. In this research, using the quantitative approach, statistical techniques have been applied to test the relationships among variables; in support, Burns (2000) suggested that the standardised test is helpful in forming an important part of the body of necessary information. Hair et al. (2010) recommended that the most common test for normality is the Kolmogorov-Smirnov test which determines the level of significance of the differences from a normal distribution. The most commonly used significant level is 0.05. Hence, the organisational performance was tested for the normality using this test. The results indicated that the significant levels of the sample are greater than 0.05 (see Table A-1 in Appendices). So, it can be concluded that the sample has a normal distribution and conforms to acceptable formats.

In contrast to the other types, external validity reflects the degree to which the samples are actually representative of the population from which they were drawn. In this study, the respondents have been stratified based on the location of their firms to ensure that each sample from the different locations had an equal chance of being selected. A probability or random sample technique was then applied to select samples. This means that the samples were randomly selected, contributing further to the generalisability of the data gathered.

In addition, the questionnaire was sent to professional proof readers based in the UK and Thailand in order to check translations from English to Thai and from Thai to English. This was necessary to ensure that the respondents shared the same understanding of the phrases applied in every single question. All respondents were also assured of the highest level of confidentiality of data, and that it would be used for academic purposes only. Respondents were also notified that a copy of the results would be provided, although no individual companies would be identifiable from the published information.

3.3 Conclusion

This chapter has discussed the research methods applied for this research. The next chapter discusses the data analysis and results.

Chapter 4
Discussion of Research Findings

4.1 Introduction

This chapter presents the findings of the statistical analysis incorporated with descriptive statistics, correlations and multiple regression analysis. The variables are gender, age, education, experience, number of employees, PKM, leadership styles and organisational performance. Finally, we report the results from analysing our data and our research findings are discussed.

4.1.1 Correlation Coefficient

To assess the predictive value of the regression line, a measure of strength of the relationship among variables is necessary. In this section, Pearson's correlation analysis was implemented to test the relationship among the variables. Correlation analysis is appropriate to describe the strength and direction of the relationship (Punch 1998). From the central limit theorem, if the sample size is sufficiently large (n is equivalent to or larger than 30), the sampling distribution of means is supposed to be normally distributed (Grimm 1993). Hence it could be supposed that the sampling distribution of means in this study is normally distributed as the sample size is 539. Pearson's correlation analysis, or r, determines the strength between two ranked or quantifiable variables, i.e. the extent to which the values of the two variables are 'proportional' to each other (Saunders et al. 2009). The following guidelines can be applied to define the strength of the relationship.

According to Hair et al. (2010), the interval scales and ratio scales provide the highest level of measurement precision, permitting nearly any mathematical operation to be performed. Ratio scales represent the highest form of measurement precision because they possess the advantages of all lower scales plus an absolute zero point. Any mathematical operation is permissible with ratio scale

© The Author(s) 2015
V. Zumitzavan and J. Michie, *Personal Knowledge Management, Leadership Styles, and Organisational Performance*, SpringerBriefs in Business,
DOI 10.1007/978-981-287-438-2_4

measurement. In this research, organisational performance was identified using a ratio scale, so it can be supposed that it provides the highest level of precision.

4.1.2 Multiple Regression Analysis

Multiple regression is one of the most recognised and widely used methods of quantitative study (Hardy 1993). A typical regression model attempts to explain variation as a quantitative dependent variable or Y, by mapping the relationship of Y to a specified set of independent variables as an additive, linear function. Observing the least squares estimation techniques could help in understanding a prediction equation and allows us to estimate conditional means on the dependent variable—expected values of Y. Special combinations of values are assessable as quantitative variables for which it can be supposed that there are equal intervals relative to an arbitrary zero point; the number of feasible predicted values for Y is unlimited. In addition, when both dependent and independent variables are quantitative, the set of relationships can be captured symmetrically.

Hierarchical multiple regression is an extension of linear regression (Raudenbush and Bryk 2002). This is used when one is interested in the linear relationship between a set of independent variables and one dependent variable. In multiple regression, the independent variables are occasionally referred to as predictor variables and the dependent variable is known as the criterion variable. Multiple regression analysis has traditionally been identified as appropriate for interval or ratio scales (Cohen et al. 2014). It is the preferred statistical method for identifying interaction effects. Most applications engage random effects designs in field settings where surveys are utilised to determine individual and organisational characteristics of interest. As a result, the independent and dependent variables in this research are ratio scale and are appropriate for application with the Multiple Regression Analysis method.

In addition, Lindeman et al. (1980) suggest that it is necessary to have a sample size of at least 100 in order to apply multiple regression effectively; and Hair et al. (2010) suggest a ratio of 5:1 as the standard to achieve to ensure that the data collected would be adequate to reflect the phenomenon being studied. More specifically, taking into account all the independent variables, a sample that is at least one-fifth of the target population size is required. Thus, the high response rate could further contribute to the representativeness of the data collected. In this study, 15 independent variables were analysed: Number of Employees, Gender, Age, Education, Experience, Retrieving, Evaluating, Organising, Collaborating, Analysing, Presenting, Securing, Transformational, Transactional and Laissez-faire Leadership Styles. Therefore, the minimum sample size required is estimated to be at least 75. In this research there are 539 cases or respondents, so it is clear that the research sample is sufficient to apply multiple regression analysis.

Sequential or hierarchical analysis of a set of independent variables may often produce the coefficients necessary to answer the scientific questions at hand. In the hierarchical form, the set of independent variables are entered cumulatively in the R^2 and partial regression and correlation coefficients are determined when each independent variable joins the others (Dugard et al. 2010). A full hierarchical procedure for a set of independent variables consists of a series of regression analyses, each with one more variable than its predecessor. The choice of a particular cumulative sequence of independent variables is made in advance, as emphasised by the purpose of the research. Moreover, the researchers should be guided by the theoretical foundation that originally led to the research question (Kerr et al. 2002). The higher the correlation between the independent and dependent variables, the better prediction equation they could provide (Stevens 2012). This research framework has three main groups of independent variables: Respondents' demographics and number of employees; PKM; and leadership styles. Thus, the relationship between independent and dependent variables has been verified to attain the results precisely, and hierarchical regression analysis has been applied.

4.1.3 Multicollinearity

High correlation between each pair of independent variables can pose an underlying collinearity problem. Pearson's correlation among independent variables or predictors should not exceed 0.8; otherwise the independent variables that show a relationship at or in excess of 0.8 may be suspected of exhibiting multicollinearity (Bryman 2006). When two regressors or X, independent variables, are very closely related, it is difficult to 'untangle' their separate effects (Wonnacott and Wonnacott 1990). Another approach, still based on the matrix of correlations, is the Variance Inflation Factor (VIF) which provides an index of the amount of the variance of each regression coefficient increased relative to a situation in which all of the predictor variables are uncorrelated (Cohen et al. 2014). Some statistical packages, including SPSS, present the tolerance (Gunst and Mason 1980). Instead of VIF, the tolerance may be its reciprocal.

Hair et al. (2010) propose that if VIF equals 1.0, i.e. tolerance is 1.0, then there is no multicollinearity in this condition. To avoid the multicollinearity problem, VIF should not exceed a value of 10. However, particularly when the sample size is smaller, the researchers may wish to be more restrictive because of increases in standard errors due to the multicollinearity. With a VIF threshold of 10, this tolerance would correspond to standard error being 'inflated' more than three times ($\sqrt{10} = 3.16$) to what it would be with no multicollinearity (Hair et al. 2010, p. 230).

$$\text{VIF} = \frac{1}{\text{Tolerance}} = \frac{1}{\left(1 - R^2_{X_i}\right)}$$

where:

R^2 = Coefficient of Determination
X_i = Independent Variables

Thus, it is essential to scrutinise the significant-level relationship among independent variables. To detect problems of multicollinearity, the coefficient correlation of each pair of independent variables has been observed (see Table A.23 Coefficient Correlation). It was found that the coefficient correlation of the set of independent variables did not exceed 0.8. Furthermore, tolerance and VIF were tested for multicollinearity; it was found that the tolerance of each predictor was not lower than 0.1 and the VIF did not exceed 3.16 (the limit suggested by Hair et al. 2010), so multicollinearity does not appear to be present. Nevertheless, given the size and cross-sectional nature of the data, multicollinearity and its implications for the interpretation of the results cannot be ruled out completely.

4.1.4 Dummy Variable

The coding of categorical data requires the development of mutually exclusive and exhaustive categories (Tabachnick and Fidell 2012). Categorical variables can be dichotomous, using binary (0, 1) coding; dummy variables are always dichotomous. All respondents who are members of a particular category are assigned a code of 1; respondents not in that particular category receive a code of 0. Following this coding convention, the researchers construct a set of dummy variables for a given categorisation so that any particular respondent is coded 1 on one and only one dummy variable in the set. In this research, the gender of respondents is a categorical variable and is recoded with male as 0 and female as 1.

4.1.5 Hypotheses

Hypothesis 1: Different demographics lead to different levels of organisational performance

H1a. Different genders lead to different levels of organisational performance
H1b. Different ages lead to different levels of organisational performance
H1c. Different levels of education lead to different levels of organisational performance
H1d. Different lengths of experience lead to different levels of organisational performance
H1e. Different numbers of employees lead to different levels of organisational performance

Hypothesis 2: Different PKM leads to different levels of organisational performance

H2a. Different types of retrieval lead to different levels of organisational performance

H2b. Different types of evaluation lead to different levels of organisational performance

H2c. Different types of organisation lead to different levels of organisational performance

H2d. Different types of analysis lead to different levels of organisational performance

H2e. Different types of collaboration lead to different levels of organisational performance

H2f. Different types of presentation lead to different levels of organisational performance

H2g. Different types of security lead to different levels of organisational performance

Hypothesis 3: Different leadership styles lead to different levels of performance

H3a. Different levels of transformational leadership styles lead to different levels of organisational performance

H3b. Different levels of transactional leadership styles lead to different levels of organisational performance

H3c. Different levels of laissez-faire leadership styles lead to different levels of organisational performance

Hypothesis 4: Different demographics, PKM and leadership styles lead to different levels of organisational performance

Hypothesis 5: The relationship between demographics, PKM and organisational performance may be mediated by leadership styles.

Hypothesis 1: Different demographics and number of employees lead to different levels of organisational performance.

H_0: $\beta 1, = \beta 2 \ldots = \beta k = 0$, there is no significant linear relationship between the set of predictors composed of Number of Employees and Demographics of Respondents, and the dependent variable, Organisational Performance.

H_1: $\beta i \neq 0$, $i = 1, 2 \ldots k$, there is a significant linear relationship between the set of predictors composed of Number of Employees and Demographics of Respondents, and the dependent variable, Organisational Performance.

Table 4.1 shows that the value of R^2, 0.259, means there is an approximately 25.9 % possibility that the independent variables in this model could explain the dependent variable. The results of ANOVA suggest that the P value is equal to 0.000 which is less than 0.05; therefore, the null hypothesis is rejected. It could be concluded that Number of Employees and Demographics of Respondents impact on Organisational Performance. Once a set of independent variables impacts on the dependent variable, the prediction equation can be ascertained.

Table 4.1 Model summary (Demographics of respondents)

Independent variables	R^2	Sig
Gender, age, education, experience and number of employees	0.259	0.000**

**Significance at the 0.01 level; Dependent variable: organisational performance

4.1.6 Beta Coefficient

$$Y = \beta_1 X_1 + \beta_2 X_2 + \beta_3 X_3 + \beta_4 X_4 + \beta_5 X_5$$

where

> Y = Organisational Performance
> βi = Beta Coefficient
> X_1 = Gender
> X_2 = Age
> X_3 = Education
> X_4 = Experience
> X_5 = Number of Employees

Organisational Performance = −0.026 (Gender) + 0.494 (Age) + 0.038 (Education) + 0.008 (Experience) + 0.097 (Number of Employees)

The coefficient beta (β) assists in determining whether the averaging process used in calculating coefficient alpha is masking any inconsistent item (Malhotra and Birks 2003). β is the standard unit of each independent variable which explains the significance value of each predictor in the equation (Auamnoy 2002). From the prediction equation above, the results suggest that the Beta Coefficient indicated that once all independent variables have been standardised in the same unit, they can be ranked as follows.

The most powerful predictor in the Standardised Coefficient Equation is age (β = 0.494). It indicated that age has a positive relationship with organisational performance. Hence, it could be supposed that the older the top managers, the greater organisational performance they can contribute to the organisation. The Beta Coefficient of number of employees is 0.097, meaning that it is another predictor which has a positive relationship with organisational performance. It is approximately five times less powerful to the organisational performance than is age, and it can be supposed that the greater the number of employees, the greater the levels of organisational performance the organisation would attain.

Education has a Beta Coefficient of 0.038, suggesting a positive relationship with organisational performance. Therefore, it could be supposed that top management with higher levels of education may be supportive to the organisation. Next, gender is −0.026 indicating that male top management may perform better than female top management, although this result may be due to response bias between genders in how successful they evaluate their organisational performance to be. Last, experience is 0.008, suggesting that the longer the lengths of experience the greater the level of organisational performance the top management can contribute to the organisation. Hence, it can be concluded that different demographics of respondents and number of employees lead to different levels of organisational performance. Therefore, hypotheses H1a, H1b, H1c, H1d and H1e were accepted.

In addition, as can be seen from Table 4.2, it was found that the tolerance of each predictor is not lower than 0.1 and the VIF does not exceed 3.16. In line with Hair et al.'s (2010) guidelines, no evidence of multicollinearity was found.

Hypothesis 2: Different PKM leads to different levels of organisational performance

H_0: $\beta1$, = $\beta2$ ... = βk = 0, there is no significant linear relationship between the set of predictors composed of Retrieving, Evaluating, Organising, Collaborating, Analysing, Presenting, Securing and the dependent variable, Organisational Performance.

H_1: $\beta i \neq 0$, $i = 1, 2... k$, there is a significant linear relationship between the set of predictors composed of Retrieving, Evaluating, Organising, Collaborating, Analysing, Presenting, Securing and the dependent variable, Organisational Performance.

Table 4.3 shows that the value of R^2, 0.416, means there is an approximately 41.6 % possibility that the independent variables in this model could explain the dependent variable. The results of ANOVA suggest that the P value is equal to 0.00 which is less than 0.05; therefore, the null hypothesis is rejected. It could be concluded that the independent variables impact on organisational performance, the dependent variable, so the prediction equation can be ascertained.

Table 4.2 Coefficient (Demographics of respondents)

Independent variables	Standardised coefficients	Collinearity statistics	
	Beta	Tolerance	VIF
Gender	−0.026	0.957	1.044
Age	0.494	0.420	2.383
Education	0.038	0.988	1.012
Experience	0.008	0.424	2.356
Number of employees	0.097	0.976	1.024

Dependent variable: organisational performance

Table 4.3 Model summary (PKM)

Independent variables	R^2	Sig
Retrieving, evaluating, organising, collaborating, analysing, presenting and securing	0.416	0.000**

**Significance at the 0.01 level; Dependent variable: organisational performance

4.1.7 Beta Coefficient

$$Y = \beta_1 X_1 + \beta_2 X_2 + \beta_3 X_3 + \beta_4 X_4 + \beta_5 X_5 + \beta_6 X_6 + \beta_7 X_7$$

where

  Y = Organisational Performance
  βi = Beta Coefficient
  X_1 = Retrieving
  X_2 = Evaluating
  X_3 = Organising
  X_4 = Collaborating
  X_5 = Analysing
  X_6 = Presenting
  X_7 = Securing

Organisational Performance = −0.052 (Retrieving) + 0.552 (Evaluating) + 0.080 (Organising) − 0.016 (Collaborating) − 0.253 (Analysing) + 0.035 (Presenting) + 0.029 (Securing)

From the prediction equation, it was found that the most powerful predictor in the Standardised Coefficient Equation is evaluating (Beta Coefficient = 0.552). It indicated that evaluating has a positive relationship with organisational performance, followed by analysing which has −0.253, suggesting that it has a negative relationship with organisational performance. Next, organising (Beta Coefficient = −0.08) has a positive relationship with organisational performance. The Beta Coefficient of retrieving is −0.052, suggesting that retrieving has a negative relationship with organisational performance. Also, at 0.035, presenting appears to have a positive relationship with organisational performance. Securing is 0.029, suggesting that it has a positive relationship with organisational performance. Last, collaborating is -0.016, suggesting that it has a negative relationship with organisational performance.

Hence, it can be concluded that different aspects of PKM lead to different levels of organisational performance. Therefore, hypotheses H2a, H2b, H2c, H2d, H2e, H2f and H2g were accepted. In addition, as can be seen from Table 4.4, it was found that the Tolerance of each predictor is not lower than 0.100 and the VIF does not exceed 3.16. In line with Hair et al.'s (2010) guidelines, no evidence of multicollinearity was found.

Hypothesis 3: Different leadership styles lead to different levels of performance

H_0: $\beta 1, = \beta 2 \ldots = \beta k = 0$, there is no significant linear relationship between the set of predictors composed of Transformational, Transactional, Laissez-faire Leadership and the dependent variable, Organisational Performance.

H_1: $\beta i \neq 0$, i = 1, 2... k, there is a significant linear relationship between the set of predictors composed of Transformational, Transactional, Laissez-faire Leadership and the dependent variable, Organisational Performance.

Table 4.4 Coefficient (PKM)

Independent variables	Standardised coefficients	Collinearity statistics	
	Beta	Tolerance	VIF
Retrieving	0.052	0.597	2.031
Evaluating	0.552	0.691	1.051
Organising	0.080	0.672	1.237
Collaborating	−0.016	0.919	1.373
Analysing	0.253	0.761	1.213
Presenting	0.035	0.671	1.174
Securing	0.029	0.871	1.313

Dependent variable: organisational performance

Table 4.5 Model summary (leadership styles)

Independent variables	R^2	Sig
Transformational, transactiona, and Laissez-faire	0.695	0.000**

**Significance at the 0.01 level; Dependent variable: organisational performance

The value of R^2, 0.695 means there is an approximately 69.5 % possibility that the independent variables in this model could explain the dependent variable. The results of ANOVA suggest that the P value is equal to 0.00 which is less than 0.05; therefore, the null hypothesis is rejected. It could be concluded that Transformational, Transactional and Laissez-faire Leadership influence Organisational Performance, so the prediction equation can be ascertained.

Beta Coefficient

$$Y = \beta_1 X_1 + \beta_2 X_2 + \beta_3 X_3$$

where

Y = Organisational Performance
βi = Beta Coefficient
X_1 = Transformational Leadership
X_2 = Transactional Leadership
X_3 = Laissez-faire Leadership

Organisational Performance = 0.529 (Transformational Leadership) + 0.473 (Transactional Leadership) − 0.019 (Laissez-faire Leadership)

From the prediction equation, it was found that the most powerful predictor in the Standardised Coefficient Equation is transformational leadership (Beta Coefficient = 0.529), which has a positive relationship with organisational performance; transactional leadership style (Beta Coefficient = 0.473) also has a positive relationship with organisational performance. Next, the Beta Coefficient of laissez-faire leadership is −0.019. The results suggest that laissez-faire leadership has a negative relationship with organisational performance (Table 4.6).

Table 4.6 Coefficient (leadership styles)

Independent variables	Standardised coefficients	Collinearity statistics	
	Beta	Tolerance	VIF
Transformational leadership	0.529	0.963	1.039
Transactional leadership	0.473	0.996	1.004
Laissez-faire leadership	−0.019	0.960	1.042

Dependent variable: organisational performance

Hence, it can be concluded that different leadership styles lead to different levels of organisational performance. Therefore, hypotheses H3a, H3b and H3c were accepted. In addition, as can be seen from Table 4.6, it was found that the Tolerance of each predictor is not lower than 0.100 and the VIF does not exceed 3.16. In line with Hair et al.'s (2010) guidelines, no evidence of multicollinearity was found.

Hypothesis 4: Different demographics, PKM and leadership styles lead to different levels of organisational performance

H_0: $\beta1, = \beta2 \ldots = \beta k = 0$, there is no significant linear relationship between the set of predictors composed of Gender, Age, Education, Experience, Number of Employees, Retrieving, Evaluating, Organising, Collaborating, Analysing, Presenting, Securing, Transformational, Transactional, Laissez-faire Leadership Styles, and the dependent variable, Organisational Performance.

H_1: $\beta i \neq 0$, $i = 1, 2\ldots k$, there is a significant linear relationship between the set of predictors composed of Gender, Age, Education, Experience, Number of Employees, Retrieving, Evaluating, Organising, Collaborating, Analysing, Presenting, Securing, Transformational, Transactional, Laissez-faire Leadership Styles, and the dependent variable, Organisational Performance.

The value of R^2, 0.774, means there is an approximately 77.4 % possibility that the independent variables in this model could explain the dependent variable. The results of ANOVA suggest that the P value is equal to 0.00 which is less than 0.05; therefore, the null hypothesis is rejected. It could be concluded that gender, age, education, experience, number of employees, retrieving, evaluating, organising, collaborating, analysing, presenting, securing, transformational, transactional, laissez-faire leadership lead to organisational performance, so the prediction equation can be ascertained.

Table 4.7 Model summary (Demographics of respondents, PKM and leadership styles)

Independent variables	R^2	Sig
Gender, age, education, experience, number of employees, retrieving, evaluating, organising, collaborating, analysing, presenting, securing, transformational, transactional, Laissez-faire leadership styles	0.774	0.000**

** Significance at the 0.01 level; Dependent variable: organisational performance

Beta Coefficient

$$Y = \beta_1 X_1 + \beta_2 X_2 + \beta_3 X_3 + \beta_4 X_4 + \beta_5 X_5 + \beta_6 X_6 + \beta_7 X_7 + \beta_8 X_8 + \beta_9 X_9 + \beta_{10} X_{10} + \beta_{11} X_{11} +$$
$$\beta_{12} X_{12} + \beta_{13} X_{13} + \beta_{14} X_{14} + \beta_{15} X_{15}$$

where

Y = Organisational Performance
βi = Beta Coefficient
X_1 = Gender
X_2 = Age
X_3 = Education
X_4 = Experience
X_5 = Number of Employees
X_6 = Retrieving
X_7 = Evaluating
X_8 = Organising
X_9 = Collaborating
X_{10} = Analysing
X_{11} = Presenting
X_{12} = Securing
X_{13} = Transformational Leadership
X_{14} = Transactional Leadership
X_{15} = Laissez-faire Leadership

Organisational Performance = −0.035 (Gender) + 0.094 (Age) + 0.023 (Education) + 0.031 (Experience) + 0.050 (Number of Employees) − 0.041 (Retrieving) + 0.205 (Evaluating) + 0.025 (Organising) − 0.052 (Collaborating) + 0.106 (Analysing) + 0.105 (Presenting) + 0.026 (Securing) + 0.440 (Transformational Leadership) + 0.359 (Transactional Leadership) − 0.053 (Laissez-faire Leadership).

From the prediction equation, it was found that the most powerful predictor in the Standardised Coefficient Equation is transformational leadership (Beta Coefficient = 0.440). It indicated that transformational leadership has a positive relationship with organisational performance, followed by transactional leadership (Beta Coefficient = 0.359) and finally evaluating (Beta Coefficient = 0.205).

Hence, it can be concluded that different demographics of respondents, PKM and leadership styles lead to different levels of organisational performance. Therefore, hypothesis 4 was accepted.

In addition, as can be seen from Table 4.8, it was found that the Tolerance of each predictor is not lower than 0.100 and the VIF does not exceed 3.16. In line with Hair et al.'s (2010) guidelines, no evidence of multicollinearity was found.

Table 4.8 Coefficient (Demographics of respondents, PKM, leadership styles)

Independent variables	Standardised coefficients	Collinearity statistics	
	Beta	Tolerance	VIF
Gender	−0.035	0.888	1.126
Age	0.094	0.384	2.608
Education	0.023	0.919	1.088
Experience	0.031	0.392	2.548
Number of employees	0.050	0.519	1.928
Retrieving	−0.041	0.485	2.061
Evaluating	0.205	0.780	1.283
Organising	0.025	0.636	1.572
Collaborating	0.052	0.859	1.163
Analysing	0.106	0.661	1.512
Presenting	0.105	0.669	1.494
Securing	0.026	0.831	1.203
Transformational	0.440	0.653	1.251
Transactional	0.359	0.729	1.393
Laissez-faire	−0.053	0.641	1.113

Dependent variable: organisational performance

Table 4.9 Coefficient (Standardised coefficients of 1st and 2nd equations)

Variables	Standardised coefficients (1st equation)			Standardised coefficients (2nd equation)		
	Sig	R^2	Adjusted R^2	Sig	R^2	Adjusted R^2
	0.000	0.534	0.523	0.000	0.774	0.767
	Beta	Tolerance	VIF	Beta	Tolerance	VIF
Gender	−0.016	0.980	1.021	−0.035	0.978	1.023
Age	0.360	0.828	1.208	0.094	0.658	1.521
Education	−0.005	0.919	1.088	0.023	0.910	1.099
Experience	−0.008	0.924	1.082	0.031	0.734	1.363
Number of employees	0.075	0.965	1.036	0.050	0.955	1.047
Retrieving	−0.017	0.894	1.118	−0.041	0.764	1.309
Evaluating	0.445	0.848	1.179	0.205	0.705	1.419
Organising	0.052	0.971	1.030	0.025	0.960	1.042
Collaborating	−0.055	0.832	1.202	0.052	0.783	1.277
Analysing	0.192	0.830	1.204	0.106	0.781	1.280
Presenting	0.082	0.946	1.057	0.105	0.931	1.074
Securing	0.026	0.963	1.039	0.026	0.925	1.081
Transformational	–	–	–	0.440	0.563	1.777
Transactional	–	–	–	0.359	0.640	1.561
Laissez-faire	–	–	–	−0.053	0.710	1.408

4.2 Mediation Testing

Hypothesis 5: The relationship between demographics, PKM and organisational performance may be mediated by leadership styles.

> 1st Equation: Organisational Performance = α Number of Employees and Demographics of Respondents + α PKM
>
> 2nd Equation: Organisational Performance = α Number of Employees and Demographics of Respondents + α PKM + α Leadership Styles

Hair et al. (2010) suggest the adjusted R^2 in comparing models with different numbers of independent variables. The adjusted R^2 is also useful in comparing models between different data sets because it will compensate for the different sample size (p. 234). Hence, in this study, the adjusted R^2 is considered for comparing two equations. It was found the adjusted R^2 for the second equation is 0.774, which is greater than the adjusted R^2 of the first equation, 0.534 (Table 4.9). This indicates that the set of independent variables in the second equation explains the dependent variables more fully than the set of independent variables in the first equation. In addition, when adding the leadership variables into the equations, the Beta Coefficient values of the PKM variables change, suggesting that the effect of PKM on organisational performance was mediated by leadership styles. Hence, hypothesis 5 was accepted. It can be concluded that the relationship between demographics of respondents, PKM and organisational performance are mediated by leadership styles.

4.3 Conclusion

This chapter described the data analysed by different statistical methods: descriptive statistics, correlation and multiple regression analysis. The results were explained and discussed. Next, in Chap. 5, the conclusion and recommendation are provided.

Chapter 5
Implications of Research Findings

5.1 Introduction

This chapter discusses the originality, the contribution made to the subject, the limitations and implications of the research and finally makes some recommendations for future studies.

5.1.1 Originality and Contribution of Research Findings

Organisational learning is described as a process of acquisition of information and its interpretation, resulting in behavioural and cognitive transformation influencing organisational performance (Dimovski and Reimann 1994; Senge 2010). It appears at different levels in the organisation and requires organisational members to participate in terms of contributing thought and knowledge (Schwandt 2005). Pemberton and Stonehouse (2000) argue that an integral feature of organisational learning is that it applies knowledge resources to improving performance; the top manager is the main person facilitating organisational members to share and transfer knowledge within the organisation (Clarke 2005). In order to prepare employees more effectively and to encourage the learning environment in the organisation, it is clear that top management need to understand their own PKM (Mumford and Honey 1992; Stevens and Frazer 2005). Hence, it could be asserted that top management are the essential drivers encouraging organisational members to contribute in sharing knowledge, and that this could further improve organisational performance. In this research, the empirical findings indicated predominant PKM and leadership styles maintaining organisational performance.

In addition, Easterby-Smith et al. (1998), emphasising that different organisations have different characteristics, proposed that learning can occur through both on-the-job and off-the-job trainings, and from the direct and indirect experiences of

© The Author(s) 2015
49
V. Zumitzavan and J. Michie, *Personal Knowledge Management, Leadership Styles, and Organisational Performance*, SpringerBriefs in Business,
DOI 10.1007/978-981-287-438-2_5

the organisational members. They also emphasised the need for future research to study different areas and provide further examples of different patterns of activity associated with learning in the organisation, other than the one investigated in their research. Similarly, Casey (2005) suggested that contemporary studies have already extended their scope to other levels of learning, which include groups, activities, networks and organisations. Nevertheless, the theory and research at these levels of learning and the links between them are currently in the early stages of exploration. It is important to note that the relationships between these lines of research need to be reinforced to build on the knowledge produced.

Furthermore, Pelham and Lieb (2004) applied subjective measures to examine the perceptions of top management in the private business sector, and suggested that future research should include service organisations to further extend the usefulness of such studies through the generalisability of the data obtained. Therefore, one of the main aims of this study is to provide further recommendations based on management practices in the healthcare industry in developing countries, drawing on research in the Thai context.

In addition, Avery et al. (2001) applied PKM to develop further understanding of organisation. They suggested that future researchers should make a point of searching for other unobtrusive performance measures to relate to the individual learning of the respondents. In this particular study, PKM and leadership were analysed with organisational performance using subjective measures obtained from the questionnaires focusing on the perceptions of the respondents. Furthermore, the relationship between PKM, leadership and organisational performance remains largely unexplored (Gilmartin and D'Aunno 2007; Jackson et al. 2003; Kristy et al. 2007). In this research, the researchers therefore expanded the scope of this research to examine the relationship between PKM, leadership styles and organisational performance, and it was found that PKM is supportive to organisations (Avery et al. 2001; Bass and Avolio 1989), whilst transformational and transactional leadership styles are consistent with investigations by Holloway (2012). Hellriegel and Slocum (2011) and Longest et al. (1993) confirm that these styles of leadership are positively correlated with organisational performance. Lastly, it was found that the relationships between demographics of respondents, PKM and organisational performance were mediated by leadership styles.

5.1.2 Implications of Research Findings

Mumford and Honey (1992) demonstrated that PKM offers top management more insight in terms of assisting them to generate a learning environment for their organisational members and developing their learning experiences effectively to transfer knowledge to their employees. In this research, it was also established that PKM has a positive correlation with organisational performance consistent with the findings investigated by Lindelöf and Löfsten (2004). Therefore, it would be supportive for top management to encourage learning in the organisation by applying effective PKM, to transfer knowledge and skills to the organisational members. Furthermore, top management may need to encourage organisational members to share ideas and then try them out in practice. Simultaneously, top management may need to take time to reflect on and gather the information (Jung et al. 2007; Lovelace et al. 2007; Nelsey and Brownie 2012; Pirró et al. 2010; van der Voet 2014).

The findings of this research also suggested that PKM and leadership styles are strongly related to different levels of organisational performance, which is consistent with the prior findings of Chong (2007) and Doyle (2014). In particular, the learning environment can be encouraged through training from the lowest to the highest levels of the organisation, as illustrated by Singapore Airlines (Chong 2007), and extended to the healthcare industry (Doyle 2014). To be well adapted to the changing business environment, top management may need to be energetic in developing their PKM and leadership styles by participating in the training programmes provided by both profit and non-profit institutions.

In conclusion, it is necessary for managers to apply effective PKM and leadership styles to encourage learning in the organisation (Honari et al. 2010; Lehr et al. 2011; Liu et al. 2003; Reeleder et al. 2006). They may need to consider improving organisational performance through PKM and leadership styles. Different PKM may create different levels of organisational performance, and only certain PKM and leadership styles may be suitable in some situations. Therefore, top management may need to consider applying appropriate PKM and leadership styles to different situations in order to sustain learning in the organisation and to improve organisational performance as a result.

5.1.3 Limitations and Recommendations for Future Research

While this study investigated the healthcare industry in the Thai context, future studies might usefully replicate it for different geographical regions and different sectors of the economy. In line with Hofstede (1993) 'there are no such things as universal management theories'. This implies that perception which may be considered as 'tolerable' in some cultures may be considered 'intolerable' in others. House et al. (2004) believed that Thailand's Buddhist religion plays a vital role in Thai culture; differences between cultures may result in different conclusions. Hence, it may be useful for future research to explore different business sectors, industries, cultures and religions.

This research concentrated on the relationship between top management's PKM and leadership styles, and organisational performance; there may be other variables helpful in developing a deeper understanding related to the characteristics of the top management in the organisation; various forms of organisational structure, management style and organisational performance, such as personalities of the top management or organisational culture (see, for example, Aragon-Correa et al. 2007; Chang and Lee 2007; Dawson and Andriopoulos 2014; Coustasse et al. 2008;

Furnham et al. 1999; Ghobadian and O'Regan 2006; House et al. 2004). For example, Dawson and Andriopoulos (2014) propose the extent to which the management authority was centralised or decentralised, and whether or not top management directly supervise organisational members.

Hence, it is clear that the form of organisational structure may also be related to the different levels of organisational performance, especially in smaller organisations where the top managers directly manage the organisation; in contrast, in larger organisations, authority is delegated to different departments, and different departmental leaders may manage their divisions differently. Hence, it may be necessary to extend research from the unit of study of this research to investigate the association between different forms of organisational structure within a company, and different styles of management in different industries.

Correspondingly, in the rapidly changing business environment, the organisation might seek for members with great ability, experience and motivation; alternatively, it might prefer employees with a better value fit to the organisation, bring about greater levels of job satisfaction although less turnover (Robbins and Judge 2012). Therefore, adding 'value' into the set of independent variables may be useful to find the relationship with organisational performance and also help future research to discover to what extent 'value' could help organisational members to be most productive in developing their organisation.

Dependence on the self-report questionnaire suggests that the magnitude of relationships between variables may require further research. To a large extent, this is to facilitate the process of cross-checking the responses given and improve its validity. Additionally, for this research, only the respondents' perceptions of PKM and leadership styles and organisational performance were measured. To acquire more insightful perceptions from respondents, it is necessary to collect data from different groups of people, other than the top management specifically approached in this research. Understanding the perspectives of organisational members and customers is suggested by some academic researchers (Liu et al. 2006; Rusnakova et al. 2004).

Although this study is the first of its kind in the Thai context, a replication of this research in the future may be beneficial to help gain a better understanding of this industry and its prospects in the economy.

5.2 Conclusion

This chapter discusses the originality, contribution, limitation, implication and recommendation. Next, the conclusion of this research is discussed in the following chapter.

Chapter 6
Conclusion

6.1 Introduction

This chapter concludes the findings explored and discusses in what manner to adopt the findings of the research reported in this book.

6.2 Conclusion

Our research reported in this book has explored the connection between the demographics of respondents (who are top managers in hospitals in Thailand), personal knowledge management (PKM), leadership styles and organisational performance. Despite the limitations to the research discussed above, our findings do contribute to a greater understanding of which attributes of PKM and leadership styles are expedient for top management, and demonstrate the extent to which PKM and leadership styles contribute towards organisational performance.

The effectiveness of such leadership styles and practices, and of human resource management more generally, will depend on some extent to the degree of fit with the organisation's overall strategy, as analysed and discussed by Michie and Sheehan (2005). The point is that if resources are put into such leadership and HR practices, the extent to which this will have a positive impact on organisational outcomes will depend in part on whether they are aligned with the organisation's overall strategy, and crucially whether resources are being put into those non-leadership and non-HR aspects of strategy. Thus, if an organisation's strategy is one of innovation and high quality, then investment in such leadership and HR practices is likely to pay dividends. If, on the other hand, the organisation is pursuing a 'low road' strategy of cost-cutting, then this might not provide a conducive environment for such leadership and HR practices, such that investments in the latter may fail to result in any significant improvement in outcomes.

© The Author(s) 2015
V. Zumitzavan and J. Michie, *Personal Knowledge Management, Leadership Styles, and Organisational Performance*, SpringerBriefs in Business,
DOI 10.1007/978-981-287-438-2_6

This might appear to leave the organisation with little guidance, in that it can pursue a 'high road' strategy of innovation and quality, or a 'low road' strategy of cost-cutting, and whether or not to invest in leadership and HR will be contingent on the prior decision regarding strategy. However, Michie and Sheehan (2005) also tested for the organisational outcomes across the different sets of organisations according to which strategic choices had been made. The cost-cutters, whilst being able to additionally save costs by avoiding investments in leadership and HR, nevertheless over the long term were less profitable than those organisations which pursued strategies which aimed at innovation and quality, with concomitant investments in leadership and HR. The key conclusion is thus that the findings of the research reported above regarding leadership styles and organisational outcomes need to be aligned with the appropriate organisational strategy.

This study has focussed on leadership rather than human resource management practices more generally. Employees more generally can of course play an important role in innovation and knowledge management, as well as in contributing towards productivity and organisational outcomes. There is, again, often a strategic choice for organisations as to whether to encourage and promote such organisational innovation. The evidence is that where this is desired as an outcome, it is most effectively pursued when combined with human resource practices that promote participation and involvement of employees. This is researched, reported and discussed by Michie and Sheehan (1999, 2003).

The scope for generating a culture of 'ownership' amongst employees in the health sector is analysed and discussed in the context of the UK by the various contributors to Michie et al. (2009), which concludes that there is indeed scope for such policies to be usefully pursued. These too would need to be aligned with the sort of leadership policies and practices discussed in this book.

Appendices

Test of Validity and Reliability

See (Table A.1).

H_0: the sample is normal distribution.

H_1: the sample is not normal distribution.

The results indicate that the P-value is 0.227, which is greater than 0.05. Therefore, the null hypothesis cannot be rejected. This means that the sample is normally distributed.

Leadership Styles

See (Tables A.2, A.3, A.4, A.5, A.6 and A.7).

© The Author(s) 2015
V. Zumitzavan and J. Michie, *Personal Knowledge Management, Leadership Styles, and Organisational Performance*, SpringerBriefs in Business, DOI 10.1007/978-981-287-438-2

Table A.1 Test of normality

	Kolmogorov-Smirnov	
	df	Sig.
Organisational performance	538	0.227

Table A.2 Transformational leadership item-total statistics

Question	Scale mean if item deleted	Scale variance if item deleted	Corrected item-total correlation	Alpha if item deleted
21	50.060	33.209	0.395	0.778
22	50.060	31.548	0.532	0.764
23	50.130	30.548	0.601	0.756
24	50.090	30.803	0.586	0.758
28	50.370	32.660	0.462	0.772
29	50.760	32.299	0.457	0.772
30	50.390	31.907	0.453	0.772
31	50.650	35.547	0.188	0.796
35	50.000	34.545	0.338	0.783
36	50.090	32.473	0.512	0.767
37	50.130	35.064	0.208	0.796
38	50.320	32.320	0.423	0.776

Table A.3 Reliability coefficients N of cases = 539, N of Items = 12 (transformational leadership)

	Transformational leadership
Cronbach's coefficient alpha	0.79

Table A.4 Transactional leadership item-total statistics

Question	Scale mean if item deleted	Scale variance if item deleted	Corrected item-total correlation	Alpha if item deleted
25	23.190	7.965	0.407	0.738
26	23.250	7.751	0.411	0.738
32	23.380	7.544	0.605	0.688
33	23.400	7.857	0.469	0.721
39	22.730	7.240	0.510	0.711
40	22.590	7.317	0.564	0.695

Table A.5 Reliability coefficients N of cases = 539, N of items = 6 (transactional leadership)

	Transactional leadership
Cronbach's coefficient alpha	0.751

Table A.6 Laissez-faire leadership item-total statistics

Question	Scale mean if item deleted	Scale variance if item deleted	Corrected item-total correlation	Alpha if item deleted
27	11.060	2.482	0.412	0.737
34	10.840	1.387	0.615	0.521
41	10.600	2.196	0.614	0.535

Table A.7 Reliability coefficients N of cases = 539, N of items = 3 (Laissez-faire leadership)

	Laissez-faire leadership
Cronbach's coefficient alpha	0.705

Personal Knowledge Management

See (Tables A.8, A.9, A.10, A.11, A.12, A.13, A.14, A.15, A.16, A.17, A.18, A.19, A.20, A.21, A.22 and A.23).

Table A.8 Retrieving information item-total statistics

Question	Scale mean if item deleted	Scale variance if item deleted	Corrected item-total correlation	Alpha if item deleted
1.1	9.430	3.323	0.505	0.801
1.2	9.490	2.778	0.668	0.625
1.3	9.455	2.843	0.658	0.637

Table A.9 Reliability coefficients N of cases = 539, N of items = 3 (retrieving information)

	Retrieving information
Cronbach's coefficient alpha	0.773

Table A.10 Evaluating information item-total statistics

Question	Scale mean if item deleted	Scale variance if item deleted	Corrected item-total correlation	Alpha if item deleted
2.1	9.600	2.500	0.604	0.538
2.2	9.660	2.442	0.647	0.482
2.3	9.599	3.323	0.376	0.801

Table A.11 Reliability coefficients N of cases = 539, N of items = 3 (evaluating information)

	Evaluating information
Cronbach's coefficient alpha	0.716

Table A.12 Organising information item-total statistics

Question	Scale mean if item deleted	Scale variance if item deleted	Corrected item-total correlation	Alpha if item deleted
3.1	9.290	2.320	0.635	0.451
3.2	9.250	2.435	0.600	0.503
3.3	9.230	3.323	0.345	0.801

Table A.13 Reliability coefficients N of cases = 539, N of items = 3 (organising information)

	Organising information
Cronbach's coefficient alpha	0.702

Table A.14 Collaborating information item-total statistics

Question	Scale mean if item deleted	Scale variance if item deleted	Corrected item-total correlation	Alpha if item deleted
5.1	9.750	6.455	0.838	0.820
5.2	9.700	6.269	0.854	0.800
5.3	9.130	6.079	0.893	0.876

Table A.15 Reliability coefficients N of cases = 539, N of items = 3 (collaborating information)

	Collaborating Information
Cronbach's coefficient alpha	0.829

Table A.16 Analysing information item-total statistics

Question	Scale mean if item deleted	Scale variance if item deleted	Corrected item-total correlation	Alpha if item deleted
4.1	8.860	1.630	0.641	0.571
4.2	8.900	1.542	0.665	0.559
4.3	8.960	2.102	0.431	0.800

Table A.17 Reliability coefficients N of cases = 539, N of items = 3 (analysing information)

	Analysing information
Cronbach's coefficient alpha	0.743

Table A.18 Presenting information item-total statistics

Question	Scale mean if item deleted	Scale variance if item deleted	Corrected item-total correlation	Alpha if item deleted
6.1	10.810	2.842	0.478	0.736
6.2	10.800	1.773	0.629	0.585
6.3	10.510	2.671	0.624	0.596

Table A.19 Reliability coefficients N of cases = 539, N of items = 3 (presenting information)

	Presenting Information
Cronbach's coefficient alpha	0.734

Table A.20 Securing information item-total statistics

Question	Scale mean if item deleted	Scale variance if item deleted	Corrected item-total correlation	Alpha if item deleted
7.1	10.811	2.843	0.569	0.726
7.2	10.800	1.773	0.729	0.785
7.3	10.510	2.671	0.724	0.796

Table A.21 Reliability coefficients N of cases = 539, N of items = 3 (securing information)

	Securing information
Cronbach's coefficient alpha	0.825

Table A.22 Table for determining sample size from a given population

N	S	N	S	N	S	N	S	N	S
10	10	100	80	280	162	800	260	2,800	338
15	14	110	86	290	165	850	265	3,000	341
20	19	120	92	300	169	900	269	3,500	246
25	24	130	97	320	175	950	274	4,000	351
30	28	140	103	340	181	1,000	278	4,500	351
35	32	150	108	360	186	1,100	285	5,000	357
40	36	160	113	380	181	1,200	291	6,000	361
45	40	180	118	400	196	1,300	297	7,000	364
50	44	190	123	420	201	1,400	302	8,000	367
55	48	200	127	440	205	1,500	306	9,000	368
60	52	210	132	460	210	1,600	310	10,000	373
65	56	220	136	480	214	1,700	313	15,000	375
70	59	230	140	500	217	1,800	317	20,000	377
75	63	240	144	550	225	1,900	320	30,000	379
80	66	250	148	600	234	2,000	322	40,000	380
85	70	260	152	650	242	2,200	327	50,000	381
90	73	270	155	700	248	2,400	331	75,000	382
95	76	270	159	750	256	2,600	335	1,00,000	384

Table A.23 Coefficient correlation

Variables	Organisational performance	Gender	Age	Education	Experience	Employee	Retrieving	Evaluating	Organising	Analysing	Collaborating	Presenting	Securing	Transformational	Transactional	Laissez-Faire
Organisational performance	1.000	–	–	–	–	–	–	–	–	–	–	–	–	–	–	–
Gender	-0.046^b	1.000	–	–	–	–	–	–	–	–	–	–	–	–	–	–
Age	0.579^b	-0.043	1.000	–	–	–	–	–	–	–	–	–	–	–	–	–
Education	0.115	-0.009	0.082	1.000	–	–	–	–	–	–	–	–	–	–	–	–
Experience	0.711^b	-0.006	0.393	0.047	1.000	–	–	–	–	–	–	–	–	–	–	–
Employee	0.126	0.105	0.070	0.089	0.061	1.000	–	–	–	–	–	–	–	–	–	–
Retrieving	-0.002	-0.014	-0.126	-0.008	0.236	-0.017	1.000	–	–	–	–	–	–	–	–	–
Evaluating	0.498^b	-0.060	0.236	0.074	0.457	0.066	0.179	1.000	–	–	–	–	–	–	–	–
Organising	0.139	0.011	0.150	-0.005	0.001	-0.017	-0.031	-0.071	1.000	–	–	–	–	–	–	–
Analysing	0.030	-0.036	-0.041	0.040	0.021	-0.021	0.186	0.077	0.073	1.000	–	–	–	–	–	–
Collaborating	-0.172^b	-0.016	-0.161	0.000	-0.270	-0.048	0.055	0.038	-0.012	-0.025	1.000	–	–	–	–	–
Presenting	-0.002^a	-0.019	0.034	0.020	-0.107	-0.017	-0.075	-0.079	0.046	0.030	0.167	1.000	–	–	–	–
Securing	0.047	-0.036	0.014	0.081	0.026	0.024	-0.064	0.010	0.002	0.136	0.027	0.018	1.000	–	–	–
Transformational	0.678^b	0.004	0.421	0.114	0.386	0.118	-0.176	0.402	0.008	0.000	-0.113	-0.008	0.000	1.000	–	–
Transactional	0.307^b	0.006	0.080	-0.048	0.260	-0.048	0.086	0.180	0.092	0.099	-0.276	0.101	0.031	0.146	1.000	–
Laissez-faire	-0.015^a	-0.010	0.005	-0.011	-0.020	0.061	0.068	0.068	0.116	0.459	0.080	0.066	0.211	0.037	-0.115	1.000

Remark: [a] $p < 0.050$; [b] $p < 0.01$

Table A.23 shows that there are positive and negative correlations between variables suggesting that there is a positive correlation between level of experience and organisational performance ($r = 0.711$, $p < 0.01$). There is a negative correlation between collaborating and organisational performance ($r = -0.172, p < 0.01$). There is a positive correlation between transformational and organisational performance ($r = 0.678$, $p < 0.01$), evaluating and organisational performance ($r = 0.498$, $p < 0.01$), age and organisational performance ($r = 0.579$, $p < 0.01$), transactional differentiation and organisational performance ($r = 0.307$, $p < 0.01$). However, there is a negative correlation between gender and organisational performance ($r = -0.046, p < 0.01$). In addition, there is a negative correlation between presenting and organisational performance ($r = -0.002, p < 0.05$), Laissez-faire and organisational performance ($r = -0.015$, $p < 0.05$).

Bibliography

Afiouni F (2007) Human resource management and knowledge management: a road map toward improving organisational performance. J Am Acad Bus 11:124–130

Ahmed PK et al. (2002) Learning through knowledge management. Routledge, London

Al-Ahmadi H (2009) Factors affecting performance of hospital nurses in Riyadh Region, Saudi Arabia. Int J Health Care Qual Assur 22:40–54

Alexopoulos AN, Buckley F (2013) What trust matters when: the temporal value of professional and personal trust for effective knowledge transfer. Group Organ Manage 38:361–391

Alvarez SA, Barney JB (2002) Resource-based theory and the entrepreneurial firm. Strategic entrepreneurship: creating a new mindset. Blackwell Publishers, Oxford, pp 89–105

Alves J, Marques MJ, Saur I, Marques P (2007) Creativity and innovation through multidisciplinary and multisectoral cooperation. Creativity Innov Manag 16:27–34

Amaratunga D, Baldry D (2002) Moving from performance measurement to performance management. Facilities 20:217–223

Ames PC (2003) Gender and learning style interactions in students' computer attitudes. J Educ Comput Res 28:231–244

Aragon-Correa JA, García-Morales VJ, Cordón-Pozo E (2007) Leadership and organisational learning's role on innovation and performance: lessons from Spain. Ind Mark Manag 36:349–359

Arocena P, Nunez I, Villanueva M (2007) The effect of enhancing workers' employability on small and medium enterprises: evidence from Spain. Small Bus Econ 29:191

Auamnoy T (2002) Statistics and SPSS for 21st century research. Chulalongkorn University, Bangkok, Thailand

Avery S, Brooks R, Brown J, Dorsey P, O'conner M (2001) Personal knowledge management: framework for integration and partnerships. Proceedings of ASCUE conference, pp 39–43

Avolio BJ, Bass BM (1995) Individual consideration viewed at multiple levels of analysis: a multilevel framework for examining the diffusion of transformational leadership. Leadersh Q 6:199–218

Avolio BJ, Yammarino FJ (2013) Transformational and charismatic leadership: the road ahead. Emerald Group Publishing, Bingley

Balnaves M, Caputi P (2001) Introduction to quantitative research methods: an investigative approach. SAGE Publications, London

Bandura A (2000) Cultivate self-efficacy for personal and organisational effectiveness. Handbook of principles of organisation behavior. Blackwel, Oxford, pp 120–136

Bandyopadhyay A, Das SK (2005) The linkage between the firm's financing decisions and real market performance: a panel study of Indian corporate sector. J Econ Bus 57:288–316

Barney JB (2001) Resource-based theories of competitive advantage: a ten-year retrospective on the resource-based view. J Manag 27:643–650

Bass BM (1985) Leadership good, better, best. Organ Dyn 13:26–40

© The Author(s) 2015
V. Zumitzavan and J. Michie, *Personal Knowledge Management, Leadership Styles, and Organisational Performance*, SpringerBriefs in Business, DOI 10.1007/978-981-287-438-2

Bass BM (1997) Does the transactional–transformational leadership paradigm transcend organisational and national boundaries? Am Psychol 52:130

Bass BM (1998) Transformational leadership: industrial, military, and educational impact. Lawrence Erlbaum Associates Inc, Mahwah

Bass BM, Avolio BJ (1989) Potential biases in leadership measures: how prototypes, lenience, and general satisfaction relate to ratings and rankings of transformational and transactional leadership constructs. Educ Psychol Measur 49:509–527

Beaver G, Jennings P (2001) Human resource development in small firms: the role of managerial competence. Int J Entrepreneurship Innov 2:93–101

Bedeian AG, Hunt JG (2006) Academic amnesia and vestigial assumptions of our forefathers. Leadersh Q 17(2):190–205

Bell AN (2006) Leadership development in Asia-Pacific: identifying and developing leaders for growth. Conference board

Bellas MDA (2004) How transformational learning experiences develop leadership capacity. Royal Roads University, Canada

Berson Y, Nemanich LA, Waldman DA, Galvin BM, Keller RT (2006) Leadership and organisational learning: a multiple levels perspective. Leadersh Q 17:577–594

Bolino MC, Turnley WH (2003) Going the extra mile: cultivating and managing employee citizenship behavior. Acad Manag Exec 17:60–71

Bowditch JL, Buono AF (2000) A primer on organisational behavior. Wiley, New York

Brown DJ, Keeping LM (2005) Elaborating the construct of transformational leadership: the role of affect. Leadersh Q 16:245–272

Brown LM, Posner BZ (2001) Exploring the relationship between learning and leadership. Leadersh Organ Dev J 22:274–280

Bryant SE (2003) The role of transformational and transactional leadership in creating, sharing and exploiting organisational knowledge. J Leadersh Organ Stud 9:32–44

Bryman A (1986) Leadership and organisations. Routledge & Kegan Paul, London

Bryman A (1999) Leadership in organisations. In: Clegg SR, Hardy C, Nord WR (eds) Managing organisation: current issues. SAGE Publications, London

Bryman A (2006) Mixed methods. SAGE Publications, London

Bryman A, Cramer D (2001) Quantitative data analysis with SPSS release 10 for windows: a guide for social scientists. Routledge, London

Burns JM (1978) Leadership. Harper & Row, New York

Burns RB (2000) Introduction to research methods. SAGE Publications, London

Bush T, Glover D (2012) Distributed leadership in action: leading high-performing leadership teams in English schools. Sch Leadersh Manag 32:21–36

Butow P, Ussher J, Kirsten L, Hobbs K, Smith K, Wain G, Sandoval M, Stenlake A (2006) Sustaining leaders of cancer support groups. Soc Work Health Care 42:39–55

Cameron KS (1986) Effectiveness as paradox: consensus and conflict in conceptions of organisational effectiveness. Manag Sci 32:539–553

Carlson DS, Upton N, Seaman S (2006) The impact of human resource practices and compensation design on performance: an analysis of family-owned SMEs. J Small Bus Manage 44:531–543

Carrillo P, Anumba C (2002) Knowledge management in the AEC sector: an exploration of the mergers and acquisitions context. Knowl Process Manag 9:149–161

Carter T (2009) Leadership and management performance. J Hosp Mark Public Relat 19:142–147

Casey A (2005) Enhancing individual and organisational learning a sociological model. Manag Learn 36:131–147

Chaganti R, Chaganti R (1983) A profile of profitable and not-so-profitable small businesses. J Small Bus Manag 21:43–51

Chan KH (2009) Impact of intellectual capital on organisational performance: an empirical study of companies in the Hang Seng Index (Part 2). Learn Organ 16:22–39

Chang S-C, Lee M-S (2007) A study on relationship among leadership, organisational culture, the operation of learning organisation and employees' job satisfaction. Learn Organ 14:155–185

Chen Y-H, Liu C-F, Hwang H-G (2011) Key factors affecting healthcare professionals to adopt knowledge management: the case of infection control departments of Taiwanese Hospitals. Expert Syst Appl 38:450–457

Cheong RK, Tsui E (2011) From skills and competencies to outcome-based collaborative work: tracking a decade's development of personal knowledge management (PKM) models. Knowl Process Manag 18(3):175–193

Chong M (2007) The role of internal communication and training in infusing corporate values and delivering brand promise: Singapore Airlines' experience. Corp Reput Rev 10:201–212

Clarke N (2005) Workplace learning environment and its relationship with learning outcomes in healthcare organisations. Hum Res Dev Int 8:185–205

Clarke N (2006) Why HR policies fail to support workplace learning: the complexities of policy implementation in healthcare. Int J Hum Resour Manag 17:190–206

Cohen P, West SG, Aiken LS (2014) Applied multiple regression/correlation analysis for the behavioral sciences. Taylor & Francis, New York

Colbert AE, Kristof-Brown AL, Bradley BH, Barrick MR (2008) CEO transformational leadership: the role of goal importance congruence in top management teams. Acad Manag J 51:81–96

Coleman S (2007) The role of human and financial capital in the profitability and growth of women-owned small firms. J Small Bus Manag 45:303–319

Cooney JP, Landers GM, Williams JM (2002) Hospital executive leadership: a critical component for improving care at the end of life. Hosp Top 80:25–29

Correa MG, Prochnik V, Ferreira ACDS, Sergio De Carvalho Vianna D (2014) Brazilian Hospital employee perceptions of the BSC. Latin Am Bus Rev 15:141–166

Corrigan PW, Lickey SE, Campion J, Rashid F (2000) Mental health team leadership and consumer's satisfaction and quality of life. Psychiatr Serv 51:781–785

Coustasse A, Mains DA, Lykens K, Lurie SG, Trevino F (2008) Organisational culture in a terminally Ill hospital. J Hosp Mark Public Relat 18:39–60

Dabbagh N, Kitsantas A (2012) Personal learning environments, social media, and self-regulated learning: a natural formula for connecting formal and informal learning. Internet High Educ 15:3–8

Daft RL (2000) Management. Harcourt College Publishers, Orlando

Daft RL (2007) The leadership experience. Cengage Learning, Mason

Dalton DR, Daily CM, Johnson JL, Ellstrand AE (1999) Number of directors and financial performance: a meta-analysis. Acad Manag J 42:674–686

Dawson P, Andriopoulos C (2014) Managing change, creativity and innovation. SAGE Publications, London

De Vaus DA (2002) Surveys in social research. Routledge, Abingdon

Dess GG, Robinson RB (1984) Measuring organisational performance in the absence of objective measures: the case of the privately-held firm and conglomerate business unit. Strateg Manag J 5:265–273

Dierickx I, Cool K (1989) Asset stock accumulation and sustainability of competitive advantage. Manag Sci 35:1504–1511

Dillman DA (2011) Mail and internet surveys: the tailored design method—2007 update with new internet, visual, and mixed-mode guide. Wiley, New York

Dimovski V, Reimann BC (1994) Organisational learning and competitive advantage: a theoretical and empirical analysis. Ohio State University, Cleveland

Dorsey PA (2001) Personal knowledge management: educational framework for global business. Tabor school of business, millikin university. http://www.millikin.edu/pkm/pkm_istanbul.html. Accessed 11 Sept 2014

Doyle L (2014) Action learning: developing leaders and supporting change in a healthcare context. Action Learn Res Pract 11:64–71

Drucker PF (1998) Peter Drucker on the profession of management. Harvard Business School Press, Boston

Dugard P, Todman JB, Staines H (2010) Approaching multivariate analysis: a practical introduction. Routledge Chapman & Hall, New York

Dunne E, Kelliher F (2013) Learning in action: creating a community of inquiry in a healthcare organisation. Action Learn Res Pract 10:148–157

Dunphy D, Turner D, Crawford M (1996) Organisational learning as the creation of corporate competencies. Centre for Corporate Change, Australian

Durand F, Dorsey J (2000) Interactive tone mapping. Springer, Berlin

Dyer JH, Hatch NW (2006) Relation-specific capabilities and barriers to knowledge transfers: creating advantage through network relationships. Strateg Manag J 27:701–719

Easterby-Smith M, Lyles MA (2011) Handbook of organisational learning and knowledge management. Wiley, New York

Easterby-Smith M, Snell R, Gherardi S (1998) Organisational learning: diverging communities of practice? Manag Learn 29:259–272

Efimova L (2004) Discovering the iceberg of knowledge work: a weblog case. Paper presented at the fifth European conference on organisational knowledge, learning and capabilities, Boston, 17–19 Mar 2004

Eiff W (2012) Best practice management: in search of hospital excellence. Int J Healthc Manag 5:48–60

Ellinger AD, Ellinger AE, Yang B, Howton SW (2002) The relationship between the learning organisation concept and firms' financial performance: an empirical assessment. Hum Resour Dev Q 13:5–22

Evans N, Qureshi AMA (2013) Organisational politics: the impact on trust, information and knowledge management and organisational performance. In: Proceedings of the European conference on information management and evaluation, pp 34–40

Fan D, Cui L, Zhang MM, Zhu CJ, Härtel CEJ, Nyland C (2014) Influence of high performance work systems on employee subjective well-being and job burnout: empirical evidence from the Chinese healthcare sector. Int J Hum Resour Manag 25:931–950

Farrell L (2006) Labouring in the knowledge fields: researching knowledge in globalising workspaces. Globalisation Soc Educ 4:237–248

Faust D (1984) The limits of scientific reasoning. University of Minnesota Press, Minneapolis

Fink A (1995) How to design surveys. SAGE Publications, Thousand Oaks

Foddy WH (1994) Constructing questions for interviews and questionnaires: theory and practice in social research. Cambridge University Press, Cambridge

Fowler FJ (2009) Survey research methods. Sage Publications, Thousand Oaks

Fox S (1997) From management education and development to the study of management learning: integrating perspectives in theory and practice. Sage Publications, London, p 21

Frand J, Hixon C (1999) Personal knowledge management: who, what, why, when, where, how. http://www.anderson.ucla.edu/faculty/jason.frand/researchers/speeches/PKM.htm (retrieved on Mar 2007)

Fred OW, Bani O, Peng W, John JL (2005) Transformational leadership, organisational commitment, and job satisfaction: a comparative study of Kenyan and US financial firms. Hum Resour Dev Q 16:235

Furnham A, Jackson JC, Miller T (1999) Personality, learning style and work performance. Pers Individ Differ 27:1113–1122

Garg VK, Walters BA, Priem RL (2003) Chief executive scanning emphases, environmental dynamism, and manufacturing firm performance. Strateg Manag J 24:725–744

Gathers D (2003) Diversity management: an imperative for healthcare organisations. Hosp Top 81:14–20

Gellis ZD (2001) Social work perceptions of transformational and transactional leadership in health care. Soc Work Res 25:17–25

Gerring J (2007) Case study research: principles and practices. Cambridge University Press, Cambridge

Ghauri PN, Grønhaug K (2005) Research methods in business studies: a practical guide. Financial Times Prentice Hall, Harlow

Ghaznavi M, Perry M, Logan K, Toulson P (2011) Knowledge sharing in ego-centered knowledge networks of professionals: role of transactive memory, trust, and reciprocity. In: Proceedings of the international conference on intellectual capital, knowledge management and organisational learning, pp 681–688

Ghobadian A, O'Regan N (2006) The impact of ownership on small firm behaviour and performance. Int Small Bus J 24:555–586

Gilmartin MJ, D'Aunno TA (2007) Leadership research in healthcare. Acad Manag Ann 1:387–438

Glastra FL, Hake BJ, Schedler PE (2004) Lifelong learning as transitional learning. Adult Educ Q 54(4):291–308

Gleue K (2002) How chief executive officers ifluence organisational learning in professional and non-professional organisations: a comparison of education, business and medicine, University of Toronto

Goleman D (2000) Leader that gets results. Harv Bus Rev 78:78–90

Grimm LG (1993) Statistical applications for the behavioural sciences. Wiley, New York

Grint K (1991) War and peace. In: Grint K (ed) Leadership. Oxford University Press, Oxford

Grünberg T (2004) Performance improvement: towards a method for finding and prioritising potential performance improvement areas in manufacturing operations. International Journal of Productivity and Performance Management. 53:52–71

Gunst RF, Mason RL (1980) Regression analysis and its application: a data-oriented approach. Taylor & Francis, Washington

Hadikin R, O'Driscoll M (2000) The bullying culture: cause, effect, harm reduction. Books for Midwives, Melbourne

Hagen AF, Lodha SS (2004) How do CEOs perceive suggested new rules of global competitiveness in the twenty-first century? Am Bus Rev 22:62

Hair JF, Black W, Babin B, Anderson R (2010) Multivariate data analysis: a global perspective. Pearson Education, New Jersey

Halachmi A (2005) Performance measurement is only one way of managing performance. Int J Prod Perform Manag 54:502–516

Hamlin RG (2005) Toward universalistic models of managerial leader effectiveness: a comparative study of recent british and american derived models of leadership. Hum Resour Dev Int 8:5–25

Hancock T (2006) Where is the health in healthcare? Crit Pub Health 16:345–346

Handy C (1995) Managing the dream. In: Chawla S, Renesch J (eds) Learning organisation. Productivity Press Inc., Portland

Hardy MA (1993) Regression with dummy variables. SAGE Publications, Thousand Oaks

Harris KJ, Kacmar KM, Zivnuska S (2007) An investigation of abusive supervision as a predictor of performance and the meaning of work as a moderator of the relationship. Leadersh Q 18:252–263

Hater JJ, Bass BM (1988) Superiors' evaluations and subordinates' perceptions of transformational and transactional leadership. J Appl Psychol 73:695

Hellriegel D, Slocum JW (2011) Organisational behavior. South-Western Cengage Learning, Mason

Herghiligiu IV, Lupu LM, Paius CM, Robledo C, Kobi A (2013) Organisational employee seen as environmental knowledge fractal agents as a consequence of the certification with ISO 14001. In: Proceedings of the international conference on intellectual capital, knowledge management and organisational learning, pp 524–532

Hetland H, Sandal G (2003) Transformational leadership in Norway: outcomes and personality correlates. Eur J Work Organ Psychol 12:147–170

Hew D, Soesastro H (2003) Realizing the ASEAN economic community by 2020: ISEAS and ASEAN-ISIS approaches. ASEAN Economic Bulletin, pp 292–296

Higgison S et al (2004) Your say: linking internal finctions with KM: about the relationships between knowledge management, internal communications and human resources. Knowl Manag Lond 7:10–12

Hodges HE, Kent TW (2006) Impact of planning and control sophistication in small business. J Small Bus Strategy 17:75–87

Hofstede G (1993) Cultures constrains in management theories. Acad Manag Exec 7:81–94

Hofstede G (1998) Attitudes, values and organisational culture: disentangling the concepts. Organ Stud 19:477–493

Holloway JB (2012) Leadership behavior and organisational climate: an empirical study in a nonprofit organisation. Emerg Leadersh Journeys 5:9–35

Honari H, Goudarzi M, Heidari A, Emami A (2010) The relationship between transformation-oriented leadership and physical education managers' productivity in sport clubs. Procedia Soc Behav Sci 2:5495–5497

Hornaday RW, Wheatley WJ (1986) Managerial characteristics and the financial performance of small business. J Small Bus Manag 24:1–7

House RJ, Hanges PJ, Javidan M, Dorfman PW, Gupta V (2004) Leadership, culture, and organisations: the GLOBE study of 62 societies. SAGE Publications, Beverly Hills

Howell JM, Avolio BJ (1993) Transformational leadership, transactional leadership, locus of control, and support for innovation: key predictors of consolidated-business-unit performance. J Appl Psychol 78:891

Howell JM, Neufeld DJ, Avolio BJ (2005) Examining the relationship of leadership and physical distance with business unit performance. Leadersh Q 16:273–285

Ilies R,. Judge T, Wagner D (2006) Making sense of motivational leadership: the trail from transformational leaders to motivated followers. J Leadersh Organ Stud 13:1–22

Jackson SE, Joshi A, Erhardt NL (2003) Recent research on team and organisational diversity: SWOT analysis and implications. J Manag 29:801–830

Jain P (2011) Personal knowledge management: the foundation of organisational knowledge management. S Afr J Libr Inf Sci 77:1–14

Jaques E, Clement SD (1991) Executive leadership: a practical guide to managing complexity. Blackwell Publishing, Oxford

Jarche H (2010) Personal knowledge management: working and learning smarter. Inf Outlook 14:13–15

Jefferson TL (2006) Taking it personally: personal knowledge management. VINE 36:35–37

Jens R, Kathrin H (2007) Transformational and charismatic leadership: assessing the convergent, divergent and criterion validity of the MLQ and the CKS. Leadersh Q 18:121–133

Johnson G, Scholes K (2002) Exploring corporate strategy. Essex, Pearson Education

Jones J (2013) Factors influencing mentees' and mentors' learning throughout formal mentoring relationships. Hum Resour Dev Int 16:390–408

Judge TA, Bono JE (2000) Five-factor model of personality and transformational leadership. J Appl Psychol 85:751

Judge TA, Piccolo RF (2004) Transformational and transactional leadership: a meta-analytic test of their relative validity. J Appl Psychol 89:755–768

Jung J, Choi I, Song M (2007) An integration architecture for knowledge management systems and business process management systems. Comput Ind 58:21–34

Kammerlind P, Dahlgaard JJ, Rutberg H (2004) Leadership for improvements in swedish health care. Total Qual Manag Bus Excell 15:495–509

Kanji G, Moura E, Sá P (2003) Sustaining healthcare excellence through performance measurement. Total Qual Manag Bus Excell 14:269–289

Kaplan RS, Norton DP (1998) Putting the balanced scorecard to work. Econ Impact Knowl 27 (4):315–324

Kelly D (2006) Evaluating personal information management behaviors and tools. Commun ACM 49:84–86

Kerr AW, Hall HK, Kozub SA (2002) Doing statistics with SPSS. SAGE Publications, London

Kotey B, Folker C (2007) Employee training in SMEs: effect of size and firm type—family and nonfamily. J Small Bus Manag 45:214–238

Kotter JP (2008) Corporate culture and performance. Simon and Schuster, New York

Kouzes JM, Posner BZ (1995) The leadership challenge: how to keep getting extraordinary things done in organisations. Foreword by Tom Peters. Jossey-Bass Publishers, San Francisco

Krejcie RV, Morgan DW (1970) Determining sample size for research activities. Educ Psychol Meas 30:607–610

Kristy T, Jill KM, Darlene GM (2007) Learning strategies as predictors of transformational leadership: the case of nonprofit managers. Leadersh Organ Dev J 28:269

Kuhert KW (1994) Transformational leadership: developing people through delegation. In: Bass BM, Avolio BJ (eds) Improving organisational effectiveness through transformational leadership. SAGE Publications, Thousand Oaks

Künzle B, Zala-Mezö E, Kolbe M, Wacker J, Grote G (2010) Substitutes for leadership in anaesthesia teams and their impact on leadership effectiveness. Eur J Work Organ Psychol 19:505–531

Langhammer R, Moellers W, Mahmood R (1993) ASEAN future economic and political cooperation. Institute of Strategie and International Studies, Kuala Lumpur

Lantz PM (2008) Gender and leadership in healthcare administration: 21st century progress and challenges. J Healthc Manag 53:291–301

Lehr B, Ostermann H, Schubert H (2011) Competence-based demands made of senior physicians: An empirical study to evaluate leadership competencies. Zeitschrift für Evidenz, Fortbildung und Qualität im Gesundheitswesen 105:723–733

Lewin AY, Long CP, Carroll T (1999) The co-evolution of new organisational forms. Organ Sci 10:535–550

Likert R (1932) A technique for the measurement of attitudes. Science Press, New York

Lindelöf P, Löfsten H (2004) Proximity as a resource base for competitive advantage: university—industry links for technology transfer. J Technol Transf 29:311–326

Lindeman RH, Merenda PF, Gold RZ (1980) Introduction to bivariate and multivariate analysis. Scott, Foresman

Liu SS, Amendah E, Chang E-C, Pei LK (2006) Satisfaction and value: a meta-analysis in the healthcare context. Health Mark Q 23:49–73

Liu W, Lepak DP, Takeuchi R, Sims HP Jr (2003) Matching leadership styles with employment modes: strategic human resource management perspective. Hum Resour Manag Rev 13:127–152

Lok P, Westwood R, Crawford J (2005) Perceptions of organisational subculture and their significance for organisational commitment. Appl Psychol 54:490–514

Longest BB, Darr K, Rakich JS (1993) Organisational leadership in hospitals. Hosp Top 71:11–15

Lovelace KJ, Manz CC, Alves JC (2007) Work stress and leadership development: the role of self-leadership, shared leadership, physical fitness and flow in managing demands and increasing job control. Hum Resour Manag Rev 17:374–387

Lumpkin GT, Dess GG (2001) Linking two dimensions of entrepreneurial orientation to firm performance: the moderating role of environment and industry life cycle. J Bus Ventur 16:429–451

Lunenburg FC (2011) Organisational culture-performance relationships: views of excellence and theory Z. National Forum of Educational Administration and Supervision Journal 29(4):1–8

Mabey C, Ramirez M (2005) Does management development improve organisational productivity? A six-country analysis of European firms. Int J Hum Resour Manag 16:1067–1082

Maes J, Sels L, Roodhooft F (2005) Modelling the link between management practices and financial performance. Evidence from small construction companies. Small Bus Econ 25:17–34

Malhotra N, Birks D (2003) Mark Res. Scotland, Pearson Education

Mandell B, Pherwani S (2003) Relationship between emotional intelligence and transformational leadership style: a gender comparison. J Bus Psychol 17:387–404

Marcel C, Rajiv L (2012) Retail doesn't cross borders. Harv Bus Rev 190:104–111

March JG (1991) Exploration and exploitation in organisational learning. Organ Sci 2:71–87

Markides CC, Williamson PJ (1996) Corporate diversification and organisational structure: a resource-based view. Acad Manag J 39:340–367

Marlow S, Patton D (1993) Managing the employment relationship in the smaller firm: possibilities for human resource management. Int Small Bus J 11:57–64

Marquardt M, Waddill D (2004) The power of learning in action learning: a conceptual analysis of how the five schools of adult learning theories are incorporated within the practice of action learning. Action Learn Res Pract 1:185–202

Marr B (2006) Strategic performance management: leveraging and measuring your intangible value drivers. Routledge, London.

Martin J (2008) Personal knowledge management: the basis of corporate and institutional knowledge management. Managing knowledge: case studies in innovation

Martins EC, Terblanche F (2003) Building organisational culture that stimulates creativity and innovation. Eur J Innov Manag 6:64–74

May T (2011) Social research: Issues, methods and research. McGraw-Hill International, New York

Mccall MW, Lombardo MM, Morrison AM (1988) Lessons of experience: how successful executives develop on the job. Simon and Schuster, New York

Mcqueen RA, Knussen C (2002) Research methods for social science: a practical introduction. Pearson Education, Harlow

McVanel-Viney S (2008) The time is now: the need to develop team performance consultants in Canadian healthcare institutions. Hum Resour Dev Int 11:307–315

Michie J (ed) (2011) The handbook of globalisation, 2nd edn. Edward Elgar, Cheltenham

Michie J, Ham C, Mills C (2009) A mutual health service. Oxford Centre for mutual and employee-owned business, kellogg college. University of Oxford, Oxford

Michie J, Sheehan M (1999) No Innovation without representation? An analysis of participation, representation, R&D and innovation (with M. Sheehan). Econ Anal 2(2):85–97

Michie J, Sheehan M (2003) Labour 'flexibility'—securing management's right to manage badly? In: Burchell B, Deakin S, Michie J, Rubery J (eds) Systems of production: markets, organisations and performance. Routledge, London, pp 178–191. (Chap. 10)

Michie J, Sheehan M (2005) Business strategy, human resources, labour market flexibility, and competitive advantage. Int J Hum Resour Manag 16(3):448–468

Michie J, Sheehan M (2001) Labour market flexibility, human resource management and corporate performance. Br J Manag 12:287–306

Michie J, Zumitzavan V (2012) The impact of 'learning' and 'leadership' management styles on organisational outcomes: a study of tyre firms in Thailand. Asia Pac Bus Rev 18:607–630

Miller CC, Cardinal LB (1994) Strategic planning and firm performance: a synthesis of more than two decades of research. Acad Manag J 37:1649–1665

Ministry of Public Health of Thailand (2006) Listings of registered hospitals. Thai Ministry of Public Health, Bangkok

Minnis W, Elmuti D (2008) Organisational effectiveness and financial performance: a healthcare study. J Hosp Mark Public Relat 18:115–134

Mirkamali SM, Thani FN, Alami F (2011) Examining the role of transformational leadership and job satisfaction in the organisational learning of an automotive manufacturing company. Procedia Soc Behav Sci 29:139–148

Mumford A, Gold J (2004) Management development strategies for action. The Chartered Institute of Personnel and Development, London

Mumford A, Honey P (1992) Questions and answers on learning styles questionnaire. Ind Commer Train 24:10–13.

Mumford MD, Connelly S, Gaddis B (2003) How creative leaders think: experimental findings and cases. Leadersh Q 14:411–432

Murray P (2003) Organisational learning, competencies, and firm performance: empirical observations. Learn Organ 10:305–316

Nelsey L, Brownie S (2012) Effective leadership, teamwork and mentoring—essential elements in promoting generational cohesion in the nursing workforce and retaining nurses. Collegian 19:197–202

Neuendorf KA (2002) The content analysis guidebook. SAGE Publications, London

Nonaka I (1991) The knowledge-creating company. Harv Bus Rev 69:96–104

Noruzy A, Dalfard V, Azhdari B, Nazari-Shirkouhi S, Rezazadeh A (2013) Relations between transformational leadership, organisational learning, knowledge management, organisational innovation, and organisational performance: an empirical investigation of manufacturing firms. Int J Adv Manufact Technol 64:1073–1085

O'Sullivan MJ (1999) Strategic learning in healthcare organisations. Hosp Top 77:13–21

Oppenheim AN (1992) Questionnaire design, interviewing and attitude measurement. Bloomsbury Academic, London

Oshagbemi T (2008) The impact of personal and organisational variables on the leadership styles of managers. Int J Hum Resour Manag 19:1896–1910

Pallant J (2010) SPSS survival manual: a step by step guide to data analysis using SPSS. Allen & Unwin, Australia

Panayides PM (2007) The impact of organisational learning on relationship orientation, logistics service effectiveness and performance. Ind Mark Manag 36:68–80

Paparoidamis NG (2005) Learning orientation and leadership quality: their impact on salespersons' performance. Manag Decis 43:1054–1063

Patton D, Marlow S, Hannon P (2000) The relationship between training and small firm performance; research frameworks and lost quests. Int Small Bus J 19:11–27

Pauleen D (2009) Personal knowledge management: putting the "person" back into the knowledge equation. Online Inf Rev 33:221–224

Pelham AM, Lieb P (2004) Differences between presidents' and sales managers' perceptions of the industry environment and firm strategy in small industrial firms: relationship to performance satisfaction. J Small Bus Manag 42:174–189

Pemberton JD, Stonehouse GH (2000) Organisational learning and knowledge assets—an essential partnership. Learn Organ 7:184–194

Pemberton JD, Stonehouse GH, Yarrow DJ (2001) Benchmarking and the role of organisational learning in developing competitive advantage. Knowl Process Manag 8:123–135

Pett TL, Wolff JA (2007) SME performance: a case for internal consistency. J Small Bus Strategy 18:1

Pirró G, Mastroianni C, Talia D (2010) A framework for distributed knowledge management: design and implementation. Future Gener Comput Syst 26:38–49

Plsek PE, Wilson T (2001) Complexity, leadership, and management in healthcare organisations. BMJ 323:746–749

Porter P (1997) Knowledge, skills and compassion? Education research and the universities. Aust Educ Res 24:79–96

Posner BZ (2009) Understanding the learning tactics of college students and their relationship to leadership. Leadersh Organ Dev J 30:386–395

Punch K (1998) Introduction to social research: quantitative and qualitative approaches. SAGE Publications, London

Ragin CC (1989) The comparative method: moving beyond qualitative and quantitative strategies. University of California Press, Berkeley

Ramasamy B, Ling NH, Ting HW (2007) Corporate social performance and ethnicity a comparison between malay and Chinese chief executives in Malaysia. Int J Cross Cult Manag 7:29–45

Ramírez YW, Nembhard DA (2004) Measuring knowledge worker productivity: a taxonomy. J Intellect Cap 5:602–628

Rauch CF, Behling O (1984) Functionalism: basis for an alternate approach to the study of leadership. In: Hunt JG, Hosking D-M, Schriesheim CA, Stewart R (eds) Leaders and managers: international perspectives on managerial behaviour and leadership. Pergamon, New York

Raudenbush SW, Bryk AS (2002) Hierarchical linear models: applications and data analysis methods. SAGE Publications, Thousand Oaks

Redshaw B (2001) Evaluating organisational effectiveness. Meas Bus Excell 5:16–18

Reeleder D, Goel V, Singer PA, Martin DK (2006) Leadership and priority setting: the perspective of hospital CEOs. Health Policy 79:24–34

Robbins SP, Judge TA (2012) Organisational behavior, 15th edn. Prentice Hall, Boston

Robson C (2002) Real world research: a resource for social scientists and practitioner-researchers. Wiley, New York

Rowold J, Heinitz K (2007) Transformational and charismatic leadership: assessing the convergent, divergent and criterion validity of the MLQ and the CKS. Leadersh Q 18:121–133

Rusnakova V, Bacharova L, Boulton G, Hlavacka S, West DJ Jr (2004) Assessment of management education and training for healthcare providers in the Slovak Republic. Hosp Top 82:18–25

Sahay B (2005) Multi-factor productivity measurement model for service organisation. Int J Prod Perform Manag 54:7–22

Salge TO, Farchi T, Barrett MI, Dopson S (2013) When does search openness really matter? A contingency study of health-care innovation projects. J Prod Innov Manag 30:659–676

Saunders M, Lewis P, Thornhill A (2009) Research methods for business students. Financial Times Prentice Hall, Harlow

Schein EH (1993) How can rganizations learn faster? The challenge of entering the green room. Sloan Manag Rev 34:85–92

Schwandt DR (2005) When managers become philosophers: integrating learning with sensemaking. Acad Manag Learn Educ 4:176–192

Seltzer J, Bass BM (1990) Transformational leadership: beyond initiation and consideration. J Manag 16:693–703

Semertzaki E (2011) 2—knowledge management. In: Semertzaki E (ed) Special libraries as knowledge management centres. Chandos Publishing, Oxford

Senge PM (2010) The fifth discipline: the art & practice of the learning organisation. Crown Publishing Group, New York

Seufert A, Back A, Von Krogh G (2003) Unleashing the power of networks for knowledge management: putting knowledge networks into action. Knowledge management and networked environments. Amacom, New York, pp 99–136

Shackleton V (1995) Business leadership. Routledge, London

Shin SJ, Jing Z (2007) When is educational specialization heterogeneity related to creativity in research and development teams? Transformational leadership as a moderator. J Appl Psychol 92:1709–1721

Shrader R, Siegel DS (2007) Assessing the relationship between human capital and firm performance: evidence from technology-based new ventures. Entrepreneurship Theor Pract 31:893–908

Shriberg A, Shriberg D (2011) Practicing leadership principles and applications. Wiley, New York

Shriberg A, Shriberg D, Kumari R (2005) Practicing leadership: principles and applications. Wiley, New York

Sidle CC (2005) The leadership wheel: five steps for achieving individual and organisational greatness. Macmillan, New York

Smith MJ (1998) Social science in question. SAGE Publications, London

Smith DM, Kolb DA (1996) User's guide for the learning-style inventory: a manual for teachers and trainers. Hay/McBer Resources Training Group, Boston

Sosik JJ, Juzbasich J, Chun JU (2011) Effects of moral reasoning and management level on ratings of charismatic leadership, in-role and extra-role performance of managers: a multi-source examination. Leadersh Q 22:434–450

Spicer DP, Sadler-Smith E (2006) Organisational learning in smaller manufacturing firms. Int Small Bus J 24:133–158

Spinelli RJ (2006) The applicability of Bass's model of transformational, transactional, and laissez-faire leadership in the hospital administrative environment. Hosp Top 84:11–19

Stefan T (2005) Demystifying productivity and performance. Int J Prod Perform Manag 54:34

Stevens GH, Frazer GW (2005) Coaching: the missing ingredient in blended learning strategy. Perform Improv 44:8–13

Stevens JP (2012) Applied multivariate statistics for the social sciences, 5th edn. Taylor & Francis, New York

Stogdill RM (1948) Personal factors associated with leadership: a survey of the literature. J Psychol 25:35–71

Storey DJ, Keasey K, Wynarczyk P, Watson R (1987) The performance of small firms: profits, jobs and failures. University of Illinois at Urbana-Champaign's academy for entrepreneurial leadership historical research reference in entrepreneurship

Su S, Lai M-C, Huang H-C (2009) Healthcare industry value creation and productivity measurement in an emerging economy. Serv Ind J 29:963–975

Suresh A (2014) Synthesis of knowledge through responsiveness, recognition, formation, attraction and retention: an empirical approach. IUP J Knowl Manag 12:53–61

Swan J, Scarbrough H, Preston J (1999) Knowledge management-the next fad to forget people? Proceedings of the ECIS, pp 668–678

Świgoń M (2013) Personal knowledge and information management—conception and exemplification. J Inf Sci 39:832–845

Szarka FE, Grant KP, Flannery WT (2004) Achieving organisational learning through team competition. Eng Manag J 16:21

Tabachnick BG, Fidell LS (2012) Using multivariate statistics. Prentice Hall PTR, Boston

Tepper BJ (2000) Consequence of abusive supervision. Acad Manag J 43:178–190

Thorpe R (1989) The performance of small firms: predicting success and failure. In: 10th UKEMRA national small firms policy research conference

Torrington D, Hall L, Taylor S (2005) Human resource management. Essex, Pearson Education

Torsten MP, Sabine BK, Peter J (2008) The impact of goal alignment on board existence and top management team composition: evidence from family-influenced businesses. J Small Bus Manag 46:372

Tower CB, Gudmundson D, Schierstedt S, Hartman EA (2007) Do family meetings really matter? Their relationship to planning and performance outcomes in small family businesses. J Small Bus Strategy 18:85

Tsui E (2002) Technologies for personal and peer-to-peer (p2p) knowledge management. CSC leading edge forum technology grant report, Citeseer

Tushman ML, O'Reilly I, Charles A (2002) Winning through innovation: a practical guide to leading organisational change and renewal. Havard Business School Publishing, Boston

Vakola M, Rezgui Y (2000) Organisational learning and innovation in the construction industry. Learn Organ 7:174–184

van der Velde M, Jansen P, Anderson N (2008) Management research methods. Wiley, New York

van der Voet J (2014) The effectiveness and specificity of change management in a public organisation: transformational leadership and a bureaucratic organisational structure. Eur Manag J 32:373–382

Vincent A, Ross D (2001) Personalize training: determine learning styles, personality types and multiple intelligences online. Learn Organ 8:36–43

Völkel M, Abecker A (2008) Cost-benefit analysis for the design of personal knowledge management systems. In: ICEIS (2), pp 95–105

Von Hayek FA (1975) The pretence of knowledge. Swed J Econ 77:433–442

Waggoner DB, Neely AD, Kennerley MP (1999) The forces that shape organisational performance measurement systems: an interdisciplinary review. Int J Prod Econ 60:53–60

Waldman DA, de Luque MS, Washburn N, House RJ, Adetoun B, Barrasa A, Bobina M, Bodur M, Chen Y-J, Debbarma S (2006) Cultural and leadership predictors of corporate social responsibility values of top management: a GLOBE study of 15 countries. J Int Bus Stud 37:823–837

Waldman DA, Ramirez GG, House RJ, Puranam P (2001) Does leadership matter? CEO leadership attributes and profitability under conditions of perceived environmental uncertainty. Acad Management J 44:134–143

Wall TD, Michie J, Patterson M, Wood SJ, Sheehan M, Clegg CW, West M (2004) On the validity of subjective measures of company performance. Pers Psychol 57:95–118

Wang Y, Poutziouris P (2010) Leadership styles, management systems and growth: empirical evidence from UK owner-managed SMEs. J Enterp Culture 18:331–354

Way SA (2002) High performance work systems and intermediate indicators of firm performance within the US small business sector. J Manag 28:765–785

Waybright J, Kemp R (2012) Financial accounting. Pearson Education, Boston

Weichun Z, Chew IKH, Spangler WD (2005) CEO transformational leadership and organisational outcomes: the mediating role of human–capital-enhancing human resource management. Leadersh Q 16:39–52

Wiersema MF, Bantel KA (1992) Top management team demography and corporate strategic change. Acad Manag J 35:91–121

Wiggins B (2013) Personal knowledge management. In: David J, Pauleen GE, Gorman (eds). Gower Publishing, Farnham (2011). ISBN: 978-0-566-08892-6 (Int J Inf Manag 33:416–417)

Wiklund J, Shepherd D (2005) Entrepreneurial orientation and small business performance: a configurational approach. J Bus Ventur 20:71–91

William ER, Robert LT, Howard TPI (1993) Contemporary issues in leadership. Westview Press Inc, Oxford

Wilson V, McCormack B, Ives G (2008) Developing healthcare practice through action learning: individual and group journeys. Action Learn Res Pract 5:21–38

Wright K (2007) Rethinking knowledge work: supporting work and learning through personal knowledge management. KRW Knowledge Resources, Canada

Wonnacott TH, Wonnacott RJ (1990) Student workbook, introductory statistics for business and economics, fourth edition and introductory statistics, fifth edition. Wiley, New York

Young J (2012) 1—introduction to personal knowledge capital. In: Young J (ed) Personal knowledge capital. Chandos Publishing, UK

Yu-Ching C, Kuo-Pin Y, Chwo-Ming Y-J (2006) Performance, internationalization, and firm-specific advantages of smes in a newly-industrialized economy. Small Bus Econ 26:475

Yukl GA (1999) An evaluation of conceptual weaknesses in transformational and charismatic leadership theories. Leadersh Q 10:285

Yukl GA (1989) Managerial leadership: a review of theory and research. J Manag 15:251–289

Yun EK (2013) Predictors of attitude and intention to use knowledge management system among Korean nurses. Nurse Educ Today 33:1477–1481

Zahra SA, Neubaum DO, Naldi L (2007) The effects of ownership and governance on SMEs' international knowledge-based resources. Small Bus Econ 29:309–327

Zhang D, Zhou L, Nunamaker JF-JR (2002) A knowledge management framework for the support of decision making in humanitarian assistance/disaster relief. Knowl Inf Syst 4:370–385

Zhen L, Jiang Z, Song H-T (2011) Distributed knowledge sharing for collaborative product development. Int J Prod Res 49:2959–2976

Zuber-Skerritt O (2005) A model of values and actions for personal knowledge management. J Workplace Learn 17:49–64